Medical Billing & Coding

STUDY GUIDE

2024-2025

Learn & Excel!

Audio | Legal Guidelines | Q&A | CPC Study Guide | Extra Content

---

Rory George

EXLUSIVE EXTRA CONTENTS FOR YOU IN THE LAST CHAPTER!

I have recently decided to give **extra study aids** to all our readers. Yes, I want to provide you with the assistance that will help you with your study you will receive:

- **This book in digital format**
- **AUDIOBOOK**
- **BOOK 1: "CPC Exam Study Guide"**
- **BOOK 2: "Medical Terminology"**
- **650 digital flashcards <u>with pictures</u> (for Anki app) are included!(50 Digital Flashcards with practical examples** of how these terms are used in medical billing and coding practice. Each flashcard describes a **different pathology or medical condition**, with a unique case illustrating **how that manifests itself and how it can be treated.** Thus, you will have a **<u>wide range of knowledge</u>** and be able to apply it to different clinical situations).

INCLUDES AUDIOBOOK!

You can track your progress and conveniently and interactively memorize the most important terms and concepts! Learn with printable flashcards or interactive flashcards on your device with **Anki APP or AnkiDroid!**

INCLUDES 2 EXTRA EBOOKS!

TABLE OF CONTENT

INTRODUCTION..**9**
The Importance of Medical Coding..9
The medical coding process involves the following steps:.....................................10
History of Medical Coding...10

OVERVIEW OF MEDICAL CODING..**11**
International Classification of Diseases (ICD)...11
Current Procedural Terminology (CPT)..11
Healthcare Common Procedure Coding System (HCPCS).......................................11
Compliance and Ethics in Medical Coding...12
Medical Coding Professionals 12
Challenges and Future Developments 12
The Medical Coding Process...12
Medical Coding and Billing 13
Medical Coding Quality and Compliance...13
The Impact of Technology on Medical Coding..14
Career Opportunities and Growth in Medical Coding 14

Use of Billing Codes...**15**
Billing Codes and Claim Submission...15
Billing Codes and Revenue Cycle Management..15
Billing Codes and Cost Transparency...16
Billing Codes and Healthcare Analytics 16
Billing Codes and Fraud Detection 17

Effective Medical Coding Techniques and Strategies **17**
Familiarity with Coding Systems and Guidelines 17
Thorough Record Review and Analysis 18
Effective Communication with Healthcare Providers 18
Utilizing Technology and Tools..18
Continuous Quality Improvement and Auditing...19
Professional Networking and Collaboration 19
Prioritize Continuing Education and Certification...19

Examples of Medical Coding cases..**20**
Example 1: Acute Bronchitis with Asthma...20
Example 2: Knee Arthroscopy with Meniscal Repair 20
Example 3: Type 2 Diabetes with Diabetic Neuropathy...20
Example 4: Hypertension and Hyperlipidemia Medication Management 21

LAWS AND REGULATIONS **23**
Health Insurance Portability and Accountability Act (HIPAA) 23
False Claims Act (FCA) 23
Anti-Kickback Statute (AKS)...23
Stark Law 23
International Classification of Diseases (ICD) Compliance 24
Current Procedural Terminology (CPT) and Healthcare Common Procedure Coding System (HCPCS)
Guidelines..24

Industry Legislation for Medical Coding **24**
Health Insurance Portability and Accountability Act (HIPAA) 24
HIPAA Privacy Rule 25
HIPAA Security Rule...25

Centers for Medicare and Medicaid Services (CMS) 25
    CMS and Medical Coding Standards 25
    CMS and Compliance 26
    CMS and Education 26
Affordable Care Act (ACA) 26
    Enhanced Fraud, Waste, and Abuse Prevention Measures 26
    Expansion of Electronic Health Records (EHRs).................................... 26
    Increased Focus on Quality and Value-Based Care................................. 26
    ICD-10 Implementation 27
    Workforce Development and Training.. 27

Federal and state regulations... **27**
Federal Regulations 27
    Health Insurance Portability and Accountability Act (HIPAA) 27
    False Claims Act (FCA) 27
    Anti-Kickback Statute (AKS) 28
    Stark Law 28
State Regulations.. 28
    Licensure Requirements 28
    Data Reporting Mandates 28
    Privacy and Security Standards.. 28
    Worker's Compensation 29
    Telemedicine Regulations 29
    Importance of Compliance 29
    Staying Informed and Current... 29

Compliance processes... **30**
    Code of Conduct.. 30
    Policies and Procedures for Medical Coding 30
    Education and Training.. 31
    Basic Instruction... 31
    Ongoing Education... 31
    Certification and Licensure 31
    Internal Auditing... 31
    Audit Scope and Frequency 31
    Audit Process 32
    Corrective Action Planning 32
    Root Cause Analysis... 32
    Corrective Action Strategies... 32
    Monitoring and Evaluation 33
    Key Takeaways.. 33

TOOLS AND TECHNOLOGY **35**
Coding Manuals... 35
Medical Coding Software 35
Electronic Health Records (EHRs) 35
Online Resources.. 36
Computer-Assisted Coding (CAC)... 36
Mobile Apps 36
Integrated Billing and Coding Systems... 36
Telecommuting and Remote Coding Technologies 37
Data Analytics Tools 37
Training and Education Technologies 37

Data management software.. **37**
Practice Management Systems (PMS) 38
Cloud-Based Data Management Solutions 38
Specialized Medical Coding Data Management Software 39
Solutions for Data Backup and Recovery 39

Tools for Cooperation and Communication..39
Automation tools...**40**
Optical Character Recognition (OCR) Tools...40
Natural Language Processing (NLP) Solutions..40
Robotic Process Automation (RPA)...41
Machine Learning (ML) Algorithms...41
Workflow Automation Software..42
Speech Recognition Technology...42
Artificial Intelligence (AI) Platforms...42
Interoperability and Integration Tools...43
CAREER ADVICE **45**
Some career advices...46
Required Skills and Competencies..**47**
Medical Terminology and Anatomy...47
Coding Systems and Guidelines...48
Regulatory Compliance and Reimbursement...48
Health Information Management (HIM) and Electronic Health Records (EHR)........49
Soft Skills and Professional Competencies..49
Continuing Education and Professional Development................................50
Specialization Opportunities for Medical Coders **50**
Inpatient Coding 50
Outpatient Coding...51
Risk Adjustment Coding...51
Specialty Coding..51
Coding Auditing...52
Coding Education and Training..52
Certified Cardiology Coder (CCC)..53
Certified Gastroenterology Coder (CGC)..53
Certified Obstetrics and Gynecology Coder (COGC)..............................53
Certified Oncology Coder (COC)...53
Certified Orthopedic Surgery Coder (COSC)...53
Certified Pediatrics Coder (CPC)...54
Certified Radiology Coder (CRCR)...54
Successful Career Paths for Medical Coding..................................**54**
Roles...**55**
Professional Coder Certified (CPC) 55
Certified Coding Specialist (CCS)..55
Certified Outpatient Coder (COC)..55
Certified Risk Adjustment Coder (CRC) 56
Medical Coding Auditor 56
Medical Coding Educator...56
PRACTICE TESTS..**57**
Practice Test Effective Medical Coding Techniques and Strategies.................**57**
Practice Test Laws and Regulations..**61**
Answers Effective Medical Coding Techniques and Strategies.................**67**
Answers Laws and Regulations **71**
Q & A WITH EXPLANATIONS...**75**
Questions on Use of billing codes **75**
Questions on Effective Medical Coding techniques and strategies **76**

Questions on Examples of Medical Coding cases 78

Questions on Industry legislation 79

Questions on Federal and state regulations 80

Questions on Compliance processes 81

Questions on Tools and technology 83

Questions on Data management software 84

Questions on Automation Tools 86

Questions on Career advice 87

Questions on Required skills and competencies 89

Questions on Specialization opportunities 91

Questions on Successful career paths 92

CONCLUSION 93

YOUR EXTRA STUDY AIDS 95

INTRODUCTION

Medical diagnoses, procedures, and services are given codes under general regulations. These codes can be used to analyze and research medical data in addition to being used for payment purposes. The International Classification of Diseases is the most used of the several medical coding schemes (ICD). In the US, medical services are billed and reported using the CPT code system. Coders are educated experts who assign appropriate medical diagnosis and procedure codes. Coding rules and regulations along with a solid understanding of medical vocabulary, anatomy, and physiology are essential.

Medical coding transforms detailed medical information into standardized, globally recognized alphanumeric codes. A medical code facilitates the efficient operation of the healthcare system by connecting medical staff, patients, and insurance providers. Medical coding uses precise, standardized language to streamline the documentation, billing, and reimbursement procedures. Healthcare practitioners may effectively interact with other parties by assigning standardized codes to medical services, which regulatory bodies and insurance companies use to determine coverage and payment. Researchers can discover advancements in public health and create focused treatments thanks to the coding of medical information.

The Importance of Medical Coding

Administrative procedures are expedited, and patient care is kept at a high standard, thanks to medical coding. Healthcare providers, patients, insurance providers, and public health organizations are just a few stakeholders who gain from medical coding. By guaranteeing proper documentation, invoicing, and reimbursement, medical coding assists healthcare providers in reducing conflicts and facilitating financial stability. Moreover, coding makes it possible to communicate medical information clearly, lowering the possibility of inaccurate interpretations, misdiagnoses, and ineffective therapies.

Patients receive fast and accurate information about their illnesses and course of treatment through medical coding. People may make more sensible financial and health decisions by having an excellent grasp of their healthcare expenses. Insurance companies use medical coding to process and verify claims and determine coverage and payments. By establishing a uniform language for medical services, coding lowers the possibility of fraud and guarantees that healthcare resources are allocated properly. Using medical coding, public health agencies collect and examine population health data.

Specific interventions are created based on trends and patterns discovered by medical coding. This knowledge is essential for managing public health effectively and allocating resources. The American healthcare system heavily relies on medical coding.

Some of its principal advantages are:

- **Streamlining the claims process:** Insurance companies can handle reimbursement claims for healthcare providers quickly and accurately by giving codes to medical services and procedures.
- **Facilitating healthcare data analysis:** Medical organizations and researchers may compare and analyze health data thanks to standardized medical codes, which makes it easier to spot trends and enhance patient care.

- **Ensuring compliance and preventing fraud:** Accurate medical coding is essential for maintaining compliance with regulatory requirements and preventing fraudulent billing practices.
- **Enhancing patient care:** Healthcare professionals can better comprehend patient histories and create personalized treatment regimens because of medical coding.

The medical coding process involves the following steps:

- **Reviewing medical records:** A patient's medical record, which contains details about their history, diagnosis, treatments, and procedures, is the first thing a medical coder carefully examines.
- **Identifying relevant information:** Then, using the patient's medical record, coders determine the pertinent medical diagnoses, procedures, and services.
- **Assigning codes:** Using standardized coding systems, medical coders apply the proper codes to the diagnoses, procedures, and services listed in the patient's record.
- **Ensuring accuracy and compliance:** Coders check their work to make sure the allocated codes are correct and adhere to any rules or regulations that may be in effect.
- **Submitting coded data:** The medical billing specialist or insurance provider receives the tagged data and requests it for reimbursement.

History of Medical Coding

A late 19th-century system of coding causes of death, the International Classification of Causes of Death (ICS), was developed by the International Statistical Institute. ICD was developed to provide a uniform method of identifying and documenting the causes of death, simplifying comparisons between nations, and analyzing mortality statistics.

The World Health Organization (WHO) assumed control of the ICD in 1948 and expanded it to encompass causes of death, illnesses, injuries, and other ailments. The need for a more thorough coding system to diagnose, carry out, and treat healthcare services arose as those services grew more complicated. Several coding systems have been created to address this demand, including the Healthcare Common Procedure Coding System (HCPCS), which focuses on coding medical operations and services, and Current Procedural Terminology (CPT). Medical coding systems must advance to preserve accurate, current representations of medical services as healthcare develops.

OVERVIEW OF MEDICAL CODING

Healthcare practitioners frequently use various medical coding systems to fulfill their unique demands. The International Classification of Diseases (ICD), Current Procedural Terminology (CPT), and the Healthcare Common Procedure Coding System are three different systems for coding medical operations (HCPCS).

International Classification of Diseases (ICD)

World Health Organization (WHO) ICD classification system categorizes the severity of many diseases, disorders, injuries, and other medical conditions. Health statistics, epidemiological data, and clinical information are recorded and reported by it. New medical knowledge and technology developments result in periodic updates to the ICD. As of 2022, ICD-11 will be the most recent edition.

Current Procedural Terminology (CPT)

Medical professionals use the CPT coding system to report on their operations and services. The American Medical Association maintains CPT (AMA). The CPT is widely used for billing, reimbursement, and statistical data analysis in the United States. CPT codes come in three categories:

- Most medical professionals' actions, such as operations, diagnostic testing, and assessments, belong under Category I.
- Category II healthcare providers use performance measurement codes to monitor the quality of their patient care.
- Emerging technologies, services, and practices that must first undergo additional testing and research before being included in Category I are given temporary codes in this Category.

Healthcare Common Procedure Coding System (HCPCS)

The HCPCS coding system in the United States includes medical tools, supplies, and non-physician services. The Centers for Medicare & Medicaid Services (CMS) uphold a two-tiered system:

1. CPT codes that have been included in HCPCS make up this level.
2. The Level II code contains alphanumeric codes for pharmaceuticals, medical supplies, equipment, and non-physician services.

Compliance and Ethics in Medical Coding

Medical coders are required to adhere to industry regulations and coding standards as well as uphold a high standard of ethical behavior in their professional work. This comprises:

- Ensuring accuracy and consistency in coding and reporting, preventing fraud-related coding techniques like up coding and unbundling, etc.
- Maintaining the privacy of patient data in compliance with HIPAA guidelines.
- Maintaining proficiency in medical coding standards and norms by taking part in continuous education and training.
- Notifying the proper authorities of any alleged infractions or unethical behavior.

Medical Coding Professionals

In the healthcare sector, medical coders are essential because they convert medical information into standardized codes. These professions need specific expertise in areas like medical language, anatomy, and the coding schemes used in healthcare.

An accredited medical coding curriculum typically includes coursework in medical vocabulary, anatomy, physiology, reimbursement strategies, and coding systems. After completing the training course, aspiring medical coders can take certification exams from the American Academy of Professional Coders (AAPC) and the American Health Information Management Association (AHIMA).

An insurance company, hospital, clinic, physician's office, or government agency may hire a medical coder. They are primarily responsible for:

- Reviewing medical records,
- Diagnoses and procedures should be coded correctly, as well as
- Ensure regulatory compliance.

Challenges and Future Developments

As the healthcare sector develops, medical coding has several opportunities and problems. Medical coders and coding systems must be regularly updated to keep up with the ever-increasing complexity of medical services and the development of new technology. EHRs and AI are increasingly used in healthcare, opening up new prospects for increasing effectiveness and precision.

To tackle these obstacles, medical coders must stay current on the most recent advancements in their industry and adjust to new technologies and procedures. Medical coders will play a larger role in the healthcare system and contribute to resource management and overall care quality due to the increased demand for accurate and effective coding. Because it offers a uniform language for medical documentation, invoicing, and reimbursement, medical coding is crucial to the healthcare sector. By ensuring that medical data is appropriately recorded, coders improve the standard of patient care. As the healthcare industry develops, medical coding will advance to meet the difficulties of an environment that is changing quickly.

The Medical Coding Process

Medical records for patients, including doctor's notes, test findings, imaging studies, and other pertinent documentation, are carefully reviewed as part of the medical coding process. Medical coders must translate essential information from these records into generally recognized codes to accurately depict the patient's diagnoses, procedures, and treatments.

The coding procedure can be divided into the following steps:

1. **Evaluation and analysis of medical records:** Medical coders must carefully review patient files to find all pertinent details about the patient's health and the services rendered by healthcare providers.
2. **Assign diagnostic and procedural codes:** Medical coders assign the proper codes from the ICD, CPT, and HCPCS coding systems based on their comprehension of the patient's medical history, ensuring that each diagnosis, procedure, and service is accurately recorded.
3. **Check the completeness and accuracy of the codes:** Medical coders must thoroughly evaluate their coding work to ensure that all codes are correct, comprehensive, and following regulatory requirements and coding patterns.
4. **Talk with healthcare providers:** Medical coders may need to speak with healthcare providers to explain information or seek more documentation if any discrepancies or ambiguities are found throughout the coding process.
5. Keep abreast of changes to coding systems, rules, regulations, and medical science and technology developments to maintain and upgrade their coding skills.

Medical Coding and Billing

Medical coding is essential to the billing and reimbursement process for healthcare. Precise coding is crucial for claims to reflect patient services and ensure that healthcare practitioners are paid fairly for their labor. The billing process starts when a healthcare provider creates a claim, a thorough invoice that includes information on the patient's insurance and demographics and the codes for the diagnoses, treatments, and services rendered. The patient's insurance provider receives the claim and utilizes the coded data to determine coverage and compute payment.

Insurance companies use medical codes to determine the medical necessity of the services rendered, examine the propriety of the charges, and spot possible fraud or misuse. Medical coding makes it easier for healthcare practitioners and insurance companies to communicate, which reduces errors, speeds up the billing and reimbursement process, and ensures that healthcare resources are used effectively.

Medical Coding Quality and Compliance

Medical coders must follow stringent rules and regulations that control the use of medical codes and assign precise codes. The World Health Organization (WHO), the American Medical Association (AMA), the Centers for Medicare & Medicaid Services (CMS), and organizations for professional coders like the American Academy of Professional Coders (AAPC) and the American Health Information Management Association all establish these guidelines (AHIMA). Maintaining the integrity of the healthcare system and avoiding potential sanctions, such as fines, audits, or the suspension of provider privileges, depending on adherence to coding norms. Medical coders must exercise extreme caution to guarantee the correctness and comprehensiveness of their coding job and to uphold ethical coding standards.

Several healthcare companies use internal coding audits, which entail systematically reviewing coded data to find errors, inconsistencies, or opportunities for improvement, to boost coding quality and compliance. The overall quality of healthcare data and the effective running of healthcare institutions are aided by these audits, which help to make sure that medical coding methods comply with regulatory criteria.

The Impact of Technology on Medical Coding

Technology's quick development has greatly impacted the medical coding industry, bringing new tools and systems to improve process accuracy and efficiency. As a result of the extensive use of electronic health records (EHRs), it is now simpler to access and analyze patient medical records, which makes it simpler for medical coders to gather the data they need for coding. Moreover, EHR systems provide tools for automated code suggestions and validation that can help medical coders with their work and lower the possibility of mistakes.

Additionally, the profession could be completely transformed by incorporating artificial intelligence (AI) and machine learning technology into medical coding systems. With the help of these sophisticated technologies, huge amounts of medical data may be analyzed, and precise code suggestions based on patterns and relationships found in the data can be produced. Although AI and machine learning cannot fully replace human coders, they can be extremely helpful in increasing the speed and precision of the coding process.

The demand for precise, top-notch medical coding has grown due to both these technological developments and the rising focus on data analytics and population health management. Organizations in the healthcare industry use coded data to study patient outcomes, spot patterns and trends in illness occurrence, and create specialized interventions to enhance population health. As a result, medical coders are essential to gathering and evaluating healthcare data, which helps improve the standard of treatment and manage available resources.

Career Opportunities and Growth in Medical Coding

There are many job prospects for skilled medical coders as the healthcare sector develops and the demand for precise medical coding rises. Positions are available in various locations, including hospitals, clinics, doctor's offices, insurance firms, and governmental organizations. Career prospects are favorable.

Those with coding skills can seek employment in allied industries, including medical billing, health information management, and clinical documentation enhancement, in addition to working as medical coders. Medical coders may rise to management positions, such as coding supervisors or managers, as they develop experience and skills. In these roles, they supervise coders' teams and guarantee the quality and compliance of coding methods within their firms. Persisting education and professional development are crucial for medical coders to maintain their certification and keep up with changes in coding systems, norms, and regulations. Numerous professional associations, including the AAPC and AHIMA, provide tools, education, and networking opportunities to help medical coders advance their careers and advance the field.

In conclusion, medical coding is an essential part of the healthcare system. It makes it possible to accurately represent medical services and streamline communication between healthcare professionals, patients, insurance providers, and public health organizations. As technology develops and the demand for high-quality healthcare data rises, the medical coding field offers various employment options and room for expansion. Medical coders will continue to be crucial to the efficient use of healthcare resources and the overall standard of patient care by maintaining a strong focus on accuracy, compliance, and continual learning.

Use of Billing Codes

The medical coding process produces billing codes, the cornerstone of the healthcare billing and reimbursement system. These standardized alphanumeric codes offer straightforward communication between healthcare professionals, patients, insurance providers, and governmental organizations by accurately representing the diagnoses, procedures, therapies, and medical equipment used in patient care. We will explore the many billing code applications in the healthcare sector in this section, highlighting their critical role in the effective operation of the healthcare system.

Billing Codes and Claim Submission

The submission of healthcare claims, which are thorough invoices comprising the billing codes for services provided to patients, is one of the main uses of billing codes. Healthcare practitioners submit these claims to insurance companies or governmental payers like Medicare and Medicaid to get paid for their services. Billing codes are essential to this procedure since they:

1. Billing codes aid in proving the medical necessity of the services rendered, which is important for establishing insurance coverage and compensation.
2. Ensuring proper reimbursement: Correct billing code assignment reduces the possibility of underpaying or overpaying healthcare providers by guaranteeing they are paid fairly for their services.
3. Processing claims more quickly: Insurance firms and government payers can process claims more quickly using standardized billing codes, lowering administrative costs and speeding up payments.

Billing Codes and Revenue Cycle Management

Revenue cycle management (RCM), which includes the entire financial process of providing healthcare services, from patient registration and appointment scheduling through billing and reimbursement, places a major emphasis on billing codes. Coding that is precise and fast is crucial for

1. Optimizing revenue: By ensuring that all billable treatments are recorded and submitted for reimbursement, precise billing code assignment aids healthcare professionals in maximizing their income.
2. Lowering the risk of claim denials because of coding mistakes or discrepancies can help a healthcare organization's financial stability. Billing codes that appropriately reflect the services delivered can help reduce this risk.
3. Finding room for development Healthcare businesses can enhance their financial performance by identifying trends, inefficiencies, and opportunities for improvement in their revenue cycle operations by analyzing billing codes and the accompanying reimbursement data.

Billing Codes and Cost Transparency

By giving patients a clear idea of the services they receive and the fees involved, billing codes aid in cost transparency in healthcare. Patients can: By looking at the billing codes on their medical bills:

1. Use billing codes to validate that the services indicated on your medical invoices appropriately match the care you received. This can help you spot any possible problems or anomalies.
2. Recognize their financial responsibilities: Billing codes can assist patients in better comprehending their insurance coverage and out-of-pocket expenses, enabling them to make knowledgeable decisions regarding their healthcare and financial security.
3. Speak up for oneself: Patients can speak with healthcare providers and insurance companies more successfully to resolve billing disputes or work out payment plans if they are thoroughly aware of billing codes and their implications.

Billing Codes and Healthcare Analytics

Billing codes are crucial for healthcare analytics because they offer useful information for examining healthcare trends, patterns, and results. Healthcare organizations can use data from billing codes to:

1. Monitoring the standard of care enables healthcare organizations to assess the level of care given, pinpoint areas for improvement, and implement targeted interventions to improve patient outcomes. This is done by examining billing codes along with clinical data.
2. Maximize resource distribution: Billing code information can assist healthcare organizations in identifying high-cost or high-utilization services, allowing them to decide confidently on resource distribution and cost-cutting measures.
3. Assistance with population health management The development of focused public health efforts and interventions aiming at enhancing overall population health can be guided by the analysis of billing code data at the population level, which can show patterns in illness prevalence, healthcare utilization, and care inequities.
4. Billing code data can provide healthcare decision-makers with information on the efficacy and efficiency of current policies, assisting them in developing evidence-based policies that efficiently allocate resources and solve urgent healthcare challenges.

Billing Codes and Fraud Detection

Identifying and preventing healthcare fraud and abuse rely heavily on billing codes. Insurance companies and government entities use data from billing codes to:

1. Unusual patterns or trends in healthcare claims that can point to fraud, like billing for services that weren't provided or upcoding, might be found by investigating billing code data (assigning higher-cost billing codes to inflate reimbursement).
2. Auditors can prioritize audits and concentrate their efforts on cases with the best chance of recovery by using billing code data to identify healthcare providers or organizations with a high risk of fraud.
3. Studying billing code data can offer insight into the success of anti-fraud initiatives and programs, influencing the creation of focused strategies to lower healthcare fraud and safeguard the integrity of the healthcare system.

The bottom line is that billing codes are crucial to many facets of the healthcare sector, including claim submission, revenue cycle management, cost transparency, and healthcare analytics.

The effective and efficient use of billing codes is crucial for the proper operation of the healthcare system because it enables communication and informed decision-making between healthcare professionals, patients, insurance providers, and government organizations. The significance of billing codes and the specialists in charge of their precise assignment will only expand as healthcare changes and the demand for high-quality, data-driven decisions rises.

Effective Medical Coding Techniques and Strategies

Medical records must be coded efficiently and accurately for the healthcare system to operate effectively. Medical coders can use various methods and approaches discussed in this section to sharpen their skills, increase their precision, and streamline the entire coding process.

Familiarity with Coding Systems and Guidelines

Effective medical coding is built on a firm knowledge of the coding standards and regulations. Medical coders must acquire knowledge of the Healthcare Common Procedure Coding System, Current Procedural Terminology, and International Classification of Diseases (ICD) (HCPCS). Accurate code assignment requires familiarity with coding conventions, norms, and clinic recommendations. Medical coders can: increase their comprehension of coding systems and rules.

1. Engage in ongoing education: Attend webinars, workshops, and seminars frequently to stay current on the latest coding standards and recommendations.
2. Make use of coding resources. Use coding guides, online resources, and industry forums to get other coders' most recent knowledge and advice.
3. Frequently finish coding tasks and case studies to put their understanding of coding systems and rules into practice.

Thorough Record Review and Analysis

The first step in effective medical coding is reviewing and analyzing patient medical records in-depth. Medical coders ought to:

1. Create a methodical approach: Establish a systematic procedure for evaluating medical records to ensure that all pertinent data is found and considered during the coding process.
2. Be on the lookout for details. Carefully review every aspect of the medical record, including doctor's notes, laboratory results, imaging tests, and other related documents, to ensure all important information is noticed.
3. Understanding medical jargon and acronyms Get a firm understanding of medical jargon and acronyms to correctly evaluate patient record data and assign appropriate codes.

Effective Communication with Healthcare Providers

Open communication with healthcare professionals is crucial for resolving coding errors, explaining unclear information, and collecting extra documentation when required.

To enhance their communication abilities, medical coders can:

1. Build cooperative relationships with healthcare professionals while fostering respect for one another and open dialogue.
2. Clear and concise communication: When asking for clarification or more information, express your questions and concerns courteously and straightforwardly.
3. Giving criticism: Discuss options for improving documentation with healthcare professionals to promote more accurate and effective coding.

Utilizing Technology and Tools

Leveraging technology and tools can significantly enhance the efficiency and accuracy of the medical coding process. Medical coders should:

1. Embrace electronic health records (EHRs): Become proficient in using EHR systems to streamline accessing and reviewing patient records.
2. Use coding software and tools: Explore and utilize coding software that offer features such as automated code suggestions, validation tools, and built-in coding guidelines to assist in the coding process.
3. Stay updated on emerging technologies: Keep abreast of advancements in artificial intelligence (AI) and machine learning technologies that have the potential to revolutionize medical coding in the future.

Continuous Quality Improvement and Auditing

Regular audits and continuous quality improvement efforts are essential for coding accuracy and compliance. Medical coders should:

1. Participate in internal and external audits: Conduct regular coding audits to identify areas for improvement and ensure adherence to coding guidelines and regulations.
2. Implement corrective action plans: Address any identified coding issues or discrepancies by developing and implementing disciplinary action plans to improve coding practices.
3. Monitor and track performance metrics: Regularly monitor and track coding performance metrics, such as accuracy rates and claim denial rates, to assess coding practices' effectiveness and identify improvement areas.

Professional Networking and Collaboration

Networking with other medical coding professionals and participating in industry organizations can provide valuable support, resources, and learning opportunities. Medical coders should:

1. Join professional organizations: Become a member of organizations such as the American Academy of Professional Coders (AAPC) and the American Health Information Management Association (AHIMA) to access resources, educational opportunities, and networking events.
2. Engage in online forums and social media groups: Participate in online discussions and communities where medical coders share experiences, insights, and advice.
3. Attend conferences and events: Attend industry conferences and events to stay current with the latest medical coding trends and developments and network with fellow professionals.

Prioritize Continuing Education and Certification

Maintaining certifications and pursuing additional credentials can enhance medical coders' skills and career prospects. To prioritize continuing education and certification, medical coders should:

1. Maintain existing certifications: Complete the necessary continuing education units (CEUs) and recertification requirements to maintain existing certifications.
2. Pursue additional credentials: Consider obtaining other certifications, such as specialty coding certifications, to demonstrate advanced expertise and enhance career opportunities.
3. Stay informed about industry developments: Regularly read industry publications, news articles, and research studies to stay current with the latest products and trends in medical coding and healthcare.

In conclusion, effective medical coding techniques and strategies involve a combination of in-depth knowledge of coding systems and guidelines, thorough record review and analysis, clear communication with healthcare providers, utilization of technology and tools, continuous quality improvement and auditing, professional networking and collaboration, and prioritizing continuing education and certification.

Medical coders can benefit from the use of these techniques and strategies by improving their skills, increasing their accuracy and efficiency, and contributing to healthcare's overall success and effectiveness.

Examples of Medical Coding cases

This section will examine several hypothetical medical coding cases to demonstrate the application of coding principles and guidelines. These examples will cover various scenarios involving diagnoses, procedures, and treatments, providing insight into the coding process and how medical coders assign appropriate codes based on patient medical records.

Example 1: Acute Bronchitis with Asthma

Patient Scenario: A 35-year-old patient presents to the primary care physician's office with a cough, fever, and difficulty breathing. After a thorough examination and review of the patient's medical history, the physician diagnoses the patient with acute bronchitis and an exacerbation of their pre-existing asthma.

Coding Process:

Diagnosis coding: The medical coder will assign ICD-10-CM codes for the patient's acute bronchitis (J20.9) and asthma exacerbation (J45.901).
E/M coding: The coder will also assign a CPT code for the primary care physician's evaluation and management (E/M) service, such as 99214, for an established patient office visit.

Example 2: Knee Arthroscopy with Meniscal Repair

Patient Scenario: A 45-year-old patient undergoes a knee arthroscopy with meniscal repair on their left knee due to a torn meniscus sustained during a sports injury.

Coding Process:

Diagnosis coding: The medical coder will assign an ICD-10-CM code for the patient's torn meniscus in the left knee (S83.241A).
Procedure coding: The coder will assign CPT codes for the knee arthroscopy (29881) and the meniscal repair (29882).

Example 3: Type 2 Diabetes with Diabetic Neuropathy

Patient Scenario: A 60-year-old patient with a history of type 2 diabetes visits their endocrinologist due to numbness and tingling in their feet. After a thorough examination and nerve conduction study, the endocrinologist diagnoses the patient with diabetic neuropathy.

Coding Process:

Diagnosis coding: The medical coder will assign ICD-10-CM codes for the patient's type 2 diabetes (E11.9) and diabetic neuropathy (E11.42).
E/M coding: The coder will also assign a CPT code for the endocrinologist's evaluation and management (E/M) service, such as 99214, for an established patient office visit.
Procedure coding: If applicable, the coder may assign a CPT code for the nerve conduction study (95907-95913) performed by the endocrinologist.

Example 4: Hypertension and Hyperlipidemia Medication Management

Patient Scenario: A 55-year-old patient with a history of hypertension and hyperlipidemia visits their primary care physician for a routine checkup and medication management.

Coding Process:

Diagnosis coding: The medical coder will assign ICD-10-CM codes for the patient's hypertension (I10) and hyperlipidemia (E78.5).
E/M coding: The coder will assign a CPT code for the primary care physician's evaluation and management (E/M) service, such as 99213, for an established patient office visit.

These examples illustrate medical coders' critical role in translating patient medical records into standardized codes for diagnoses, procedures, and treatments. Accurate and efficient coding is essential for the proper functioning of the healthcare system, ensuring clear communication among healthcare providers, patients, insurance companies, and government agencies, facilitating appropriate reimbursement, and the effective management of healthcare resources.

LAWS AND REGULATIONS

A complicated web of laws and regulations governs medical-legal coding in the US. These laws and regulations safeguard patient privacy, prevent fraud, and ensure proper data management. Medical coders, healthcare providers, and insurance companies must understand and follow these regulations to maintain the integrity of the healthcare system. In this section, we discuss the laws and regulations that govern medical coding in the US.

Health Insurance Portability and Accountability Act (HIPAA)

The federal law, the Health Insurance Portability and Accountability Act (HIPAA) of 1996, established national guidelines for protecting private patient health information. HIPAA's Privacy Rule governs protected health information (PHI) use and disclosure, while the Security Rule establishes requirements for securing electronic PHI. Medical coders ensure that the coded data they handle conform with HIPAA's privacy and security standards.

In addition, HIPAA requires that all electronic healthcare transactions, including medical coding, billing, and claims processing, use standardized codes and formats. HIPAA-compliant code sets, such as the International Classification of Diseases (ICD), Current Procedural Terminology (CPT), and Healthcare Common Procedure Coding System, must be used by healthcare providers and insurance firms (HCPCS).

False Claims Act (FCA)

A federal statute known as the False Claims Act (FCA) forbids submitting fictitious or fraudulent claims to the government for reimbursement, including for the Medicare and Medicaid programs. Accurate medical coding ensures that healthcare practitioners bill for good services and obtain valid rebates, which are essential for preventing bogus claims. Medical coders must follow stringent coding standards and ensure their work is free of mistakes or misrepresentations that can result in unethical billing procedures.

Anti-Kickback Statute (AKS)

A federal law known as the Anti-Kickback Statute (AKS) forbids the exchange of any payment for eligible patient referrals for federally financed healthcare programs like Medicare and Medicaid. The AKS emphasizes the significance of accurate and moral coding methods even though it has no direct bearing on medical coding. Medical coders must avoid participating in any potential kickback schemes because doing so could subject healthcare organizations and clinicians to harsh fines.

Stark Law

Federal legislation called the Stark Law, commonly called the Physician Self-Referral Law, forbids doctors from recommending Medicare and Medicaid patients to organizations with which they have a business relationship to get specific medical services. The Stark Law highlights the necessity of ethical coding techniques, much like the AKS. Medical coders are required to maintain objectivity and make sure that their job does not lead to violations of the Stark Law.

International Classification of Diseases (ICD) Compliance

The Centers for Medicare and Medicaid Services (CMS) and the National Center for Health Statistics (NCHS) have modified the World Health Organization's (WHO) International Classification of Diseases (ICD) coding system for use in the United States (NCHS). To ensure accurate and consistent reporting of diagnoses and inpatient operations, medical coders must adhere to the approved ICD coding criteria. If these rules are not followed, there may be improper reimbursement or potential coding-related audits and fines.

Current Procedural Terminology (CPT) and Healthcare Common Procedure Coding System (HCPCS) Guidelines

The American Medical Association (AMA) created the Current Procedural Terminology (CPT) coding system to define medical operations and services. Medical coders must adhere to the CPT coding conventions and guidelines to guarantee accurate and consistent reporting of procedures. The CPT codes are a component of the Centers for Medicare and Medicaid Services (CMS) Healthcare Common Procedure Coding System (HCPCS), which also has other codes for services and supplies not covered by the CPT.

Medical coders must follow the rules and specifications outlined by the CPT and HCPCS coding systems to comply with the reimbursement policies of public and commercial payers. Failure to follow these rules may result in reimbursement rejections, audits, or potential legal repercussions.

In conclusion, by guaranteeing adherence to the many laws and regulations governing medical coding, medical coders serve a crucial role in preserving the integrity of the healthcare system. Medical coders help to prevent fraud, safeguard patient privacy, and handle healthcare data effectively by following tight coding requirements and upholding ethical coding practices. Medical coders must keep up with regulatory changes and business best practices as the healthcare landscape changes to preserve their competence and contribute significantly to the American healthcare system.

Industry Legislation for Medical Coding

Several laws, regulations, and industry standards intended to guarantee patient health information's accuracy, consistency, and confidentiality tightly control the medical coding profession. Medical coders must be thoroughly aware of these standards to maintain compliance and best practices in the healthcare sector. The Health Insurance Portability and Accountability Act (HIPAA), the International Classification of Diseases (ICD), the Current Procedural Terminology (CPT), and the Healthcare Common Procedure Coding System are just a few of the significant industry laws that have an impact on medical coding that are covered in this section(HCPCS).

Health Insurance Portability and Accountability Act (HIPAA)

HIPAA, a significant federal law passed in 1996, protects the confidentiality and security of patient medical records and other personal health information. It establishes a framework for protecting sensitive patient data and specifies criteria for electronic health information exchange. HIPAA's Privacy Rule and Security Rules must be followed by medical coders to safeguard the confidentiality and integrity of patient data.

HIPAA Privacy Rule

The Privacy Rule establishes the benchmark for securing patient medical records and private health data. It provides people's rights surrounding their health information and controls how covered entities, including healthcare providers, health plans, and clearinghouses, can disclose and utilize it. The Privacy Rule's main provisions are as follows:

- According to the minimum requirement, only the bare minimum of protected health information (PHI) shall be disclosed or used for a particular purpose.
- Notification of Privacy Practices: Covered entities must give patients a notice outlining their privacy policies and the rights of patients.
- Requirements for authorization: Typically, PHI cannot be released without patient consent, except for uses related to treatment, payment, or healthcare operations.

HIPAA Security Rule

The Security Rule, which applies to healthcare providers, health plans, and clearinghouses that transfer health information electronically, specifies criteria for protecting electronic PHI (ePHI). It mandates that administrative, physical, and technical measures be put in place by covered entities to guarantee the privacy, availability, and integrity of ePHI. The Security Rule's main clauses include the following:

- Risk assessment: To find possible threats and weaknesses to ePHI, covered companies must undertake a risk assessment.
- Policies and procedures for handling security risks and preventing unauthorized access, use, or disclosure of ePHI should be established by covered companies.
- Training and awareness: Employees must be aware of their roles and responsibilities in preserving the security of ePHI. They must also get training on security policies and procedures.

Centers for Medicare and Medicaid Services (CMS)

The Children's Health Insurance Program (CHIP), the Health Insurance Marketplace, and other health-related initiatives are all administered and supervised by the Centers for Medicare and Medicaid Services (CMS), a federal organization housed within the US Department of Health and Human Services (HHS). Medical coding procedures in the United States are primarily regulated and standardized thanks to CMS.

CMS and Medical Coding Standards

CMS has set particular coding standards and guidelines to promote uniformity and accuracy in the reporting of medical diagnoses, procedures, and services. The International Classification of Diseases (ICD), Current Procedural Terminology (CPT), and Healthcare Common Procedure Coding System are some examples of these coding systems (HCPCS).

These coding systems are updated and maintained by CMS in collaboration with other organizations like the National Center for Health Statistics (NCHS) and the American Medical Association (AMA). To ensure accurate reporting and compensation for healthcare services, medical coders must abide by the coding standards established by CMS.

CMS and Compliance

CMS creates rules and regulations for medical coding compliance to stop fraud, waste, and abuse within the healthcare system. To ensure the integrity of the medical coding process and prevent potential penalties, healthcare practitioners and medical coders must abide by these rules. The creation and execution of medical coding audits, launching the National Correct Coding Initiative (NCCI), and releasing guidelines on compliance and ethics for healthcare providers are essential CMS compliance projects.

CMS and Education

For healthcare providers, medical coders, and other stakeholders, CMS offers resources and training materials to support proper medical coding procedures and encourage adherence to industry legislation. These resources address various medical coding, billing, and reimbursement topics and include information sheets, webinars, and other training tools.

Affordable Care Act (ACA)

Obamacare, often known as the Affordable Care Act (ACA), was enacted in 2010. While expanding access to affordable health insurance is the main objective of the ACA, it also has rules that have a direct bearing on the medical coding sector. The main elements of the ACA that impact medical coding standards and practices will be covered in this section.

Enhanced Fraud, Waste, and Abuse Prevention Measures

The ACA has stepped up efforts to thwart waste, fraud, and abuse in the healthcare sector. It has also mandated the use of uniform coding and reporting systems and increased financing for efforts to prevent fraud. Medical coders must exercise caution in their coding procedures to ensure accuracy and avoid dishonest coding methods like upcoding or unbundling.

Expansion of Electronic Health Records (EHRs)

The ACA supports the use of health information technology in meaningful ways and encourages the implementation of Electronic Health Records (EHRs). As a result, there is an increasing demand for medical coders that can effectively record and report health information electronically and are adept at navigating EHR systems. Medical coders need to know how to use EHR systems and be aware of their responsibility for maintaining the accuracy and security of electronic patient data.

Increased Focus on Quality and Value-Based Care

By emphasizing the quality of care and patient outcomes, the value-based care model has replaced the fee-for-service model as the industry's primary focus due to the Affordable Care Act. While accurate diagnosis and procedure coding and reporting directly affect quality metrics and reimbursement rates, medical coders are essential to this transformation. Medical coders need to understand the reporting of quality measures and the significance of accurate coding in value-based care.

ICD-10 Implementation

By imposing a deadline for healthcare providers, health plans, and clearinghouses to comply, the ACA has sped up the switch from ICD-9 to ICD-10 coding systems. The ICD-10 system provides a higher level of detail and granularity in classification, enabling better patient care and outcomes tracking. Medical coders must be knowledgeable about the ICD-10-CM and ICD-10-PCS coding systems and keep up with any updates or changes to the rules and codes.

Workforce Development and Training

The ACA is aware of the value of a qualified healthcare workforce, which includes medical coders. The law has provided funds for projects and training programs designed to create a skilled workforce in the healthcare sector. Medical coders should take advantage of these chances to improve their abilities, keep their certifications current, and keep up with technological advancements and legislative changes.

Conclusion: The Affordable Care Act has significantly impacted medical coding standards and practices. By being aware of and following the changes made by the ACA, medical coders can maintain compliance, promote correct coding and reporting, and contribute to the overall improvement of the healthcare system.

Federal and state regulations

Medical coders ensure that diagnoses, procedures, and services are correctly categorized and reported for financial and statistical purposes. Therefore, the laws governing the medical coding industry are relevant to medical coders. Medical coding is affected by federal and state laws such as the Health Insurance Portability and Accountability Act (HIPAA), the False Claims Act (FCA), the Anti-Kickback Statute (AKS), and the Stark Law. Regulations and laws govern medical-legal coding in the United States. These laws and regulations protect data management and fraud prevention. Medical coders, healthcare providers, and insurance companies should understand and follow these regulations to maintain the integrity of the healthcare system. This section discusses the laws and regulations governing medical coding in the US.

Federal Regulations

Health Insurance Portability and Accountability Act (HIPAA)

HIPAA is a crucial federal statute that protects the confidentiality and privacy of patients' medical records and personal health information, as was covered in part above. Medical coders must follow the privacy and security requirements of HIPAA to protect patient data's confidentiality and accuracy. Medical coders confirm their compliance with federal laws in this way, helping safeguard patients' rights.

False Claims Act (FCA)

A federal statute known as the False Claims Act (FCA) forbids submitting false or fraudulent claims to the government for reimbursement. This refers to offering incorrect or fraudulent codes for diagnoses, operations, or services in the context of medical coding. To avoid breaking the FCA, medical coders must guarantee the integrity and correctness of the codes they issue. Severe financial fines and potential exclusion from government healthcare programs are possible consequences of violations.

Anti-Kickback Statute (AKS)

A federal law known as the Anti-Kickback Statute (AKS) forbids exchanging anything of value in exchange for referrals or recommendations for treatments covered by Medicare or Medicaid, or other federal healthcare programs. Medical coders should be aware of the law's consequences even though the AKS primarily targets healthcare professionals since they may encounter circumstances where unethical financial incentives may influence coding techniques. Medical coders help stop fraud and abuse in the healthcare sector by upholding ethical coding norms and reporting suspected infractions.

Stark Law

A federal law known as the Stark Law, called the Physician Self-Referral Law, forbids doctors from recommending Medicare or Medicaid patients for specific designated health services (DHS) to a company in which they or a member of their immediate family owns stock. Although proper coding and reporting are necessary for compliance with this law, medical coders should be conversant with the Stark Law and its exceptions.

State Regulations

Medical coders need to know state-specific laws that affect their line of work and federal laws. While these laws may differ from one state to the following, several recurring themes include the need for licenses, data reporting requirements, and privacy and security restrictions. This section gives a broad overview of state laws; nevertheless, medical coders should contact the regulatory bodies in their states for information on particular rules and regulations.

Licensure Requirements

To practice in their state, medical coders may need to receive a license or certification from that state. It may be necessary to pass a state-administered exam, complete a recognized medical coding program, and maintain a certain number of continuing education credits to obtain a license. Medical coders should become familiar with their state's licensing regulations and ensure they meet them to practice lawfully.

Data Reporting Mandates

State regulations may force healthcare providers to disclose certain health information or statistical data to state agencies for quality improvement programs, public health surveillance, or other purposes. Medical coders must know these reporting standards and ensure that the necessary data is submitted accurately and on time.

Privacy and Security Standards

Although HIPAA establishes the federal baseline for privacy and security regulations, some states have passed legislation to safeguard patient health information better. Patient data use, disclosure, and storage may be subject to extra obligations or limitations due to specific state-specific rules. Medical coders should be aware of their state's privacy and security laws and ensure they abide by them as well as HIPAA's privacy and security rules.

Worker's Compensation

Employees who sustain work-related illnesses or injuries are given medical care and lost wages under the state-mandated insurance scheme known as worker's compensation. Medical coders must understand the particular coding, billing, and reporting requirements for their state's worker's compensation program because each state has its unique program. This could involve submitting exceptional data items or using state-specific billing forms.

Telemedicine Regulations

In recent years, telemedicine—or the provision of medical treatments via telecommunications technology—has grown in popularity. Medical coders must be aware of the coding and billing standards for telemedicine services in their jurisdiction because state laws on the subject vary greatly. This may involve appropriately reporting telemedicine contacts using particular modifiers or place-of-service codes.

Importance of Compliance

Medical coders must conform to federal and state rules since failing can result in considerable financial penalties, legal repercussions, and reputational harm to the healthcare business. Medical coders can help assure their organization's compliance and contribute to the general integrity of the healthcare system by having full awareness of the pertinent legislation and staying current with developments in the industry.

Staying Informed and Current

Medical coders must be aware of revisions and modifications because laws and industry standards are prone to change. Here are some tips for remaining up to date:

- Attending conferences or seminars in the sector and participating in continuing education programs.
- Registering for industry magazines, blogs, or newsletters.
- Joining organizations that offer information and networking opportunities, including the American Health Information Management Association (AHIMA) or the American Academy of Professional Coders (AAPC).
- Keeping track of regulatory agency updates, such as those from CMS, HHS, or state health departments.

Medical coders must have a thorough awareness of federal and state rules to preserve compliance and guarantee the accurate and ethical coding and reporting of health information. Medical coders can traverse the complicated regulatory environment and contribute to the practical and transparent operation of the healthcare industry by being familiar with the essential rules, such as HIPAA, the FCA, the AKS, the Stark Law, and state-specific standards. Medical coders must adhere to ethical coding principles and stay up-to-date on industry changes to succeed and advance in their careers.

Compliance processes

Compliance with federal and state standards is essential for healthcare businesses to operate morally and effectively. Medical coders play a crucial role in this process by consistently and accurately coding diagnoses, procedures, and services.

This chapter examines the main components of a robust medical coding compliance program, including policies and procedures, instruction and training, internal auditing, and corrective action planning. Implementing these systems can reduce the risk of noncompliance among medical coders, reduce fraud and abuse in healthcare, and improve the general integrity of the healthcare system.

The basis of any successful compliance program is the establishment of comprehensive policies and procedures outlining the duties and responsibilities of medical coders.

Code of Conduct

The rules for appropriate conduct are established in a code of conduct, which outlines the principles that form the foundation of the organization's culture. A code of conduct ought to be customized to the particular requirements and objectives of the business and should cover essential topics like:

- Dedication to precise and moral coding techniques
- Observance of national and local laws, such as HIPAA, the FCA, the AKS, and the Stark Law
- Protecting the confidentiality and privacy of patients
- Reporting alleged fraud, abuse, or other offenses
- Retaliation against anyone who raises issues in good faith is forbidden

Policies and Procedures for Medical Coding

Specific policies and procedures should be created to direct medical coding practices within the organization. These regulations should cover the following:

- Standards and guidelines for coding, including the usage of ICD, CPT, and HCPCS codes
- Criteria for providing proper code documentation
- Procedures for maintaining and updating coding resources, including software, codebooks, and reference materials
- Workflows and duties for coding, such as coordinating with doctors and other healthcare professionals
- Methods for billing and reimbursement, such as submitting claims and managing rejections or appeals
- Using and disclosing protected health information following state and federal laws, including HIPAA
- Medical record preservation and disposal, as well as coding documents

Education and Training

Medical coders must maintain their proficiency in coding standards, business best practices, and legal requirements, which require ongoing education and training.

Basic Instruction

Medical coders should receive a thorough orientation to the organization's rules and processes, coding standards, and documentation requirements. Coders should receive training customized to their job responsibilities, including valuable, hands-on activities that let them apply their knowledge and skills in realistic settings.

Ongoing Education

Medical coders should take part in continuing education courses like these to stay updated on industry changes and keep their certifications.

- Professional organizations such as AHIMA or AAPC may offer webinars, seminars, or conferences.
- Accredited educational institutions may also offer in-person or online courses.
- Internal workshops or training sessions led by coding supervisors or the organization's compliance department

Certification and Licensure

As their state or employment requires, medical coders should maintain their professional qualifications or licensure. Achieving and keeping credentials like the Certified Professional Coder (CPC), Certified Coding Specialist (CCS), or Registered Health Information Technician (RHIT), as well as fulfilling any continuing education requirements related to these certifications, may be part of this.

Internal Auditing

An efficient compliance program must include internal audits because they help firms evaluate the precision and consistency of their coding procedures and spot any potential noncompliance red flags. Frequent audits can assure regulatory compliance, help find errors, and lower the possibility of fraudulent coding.

Audit Scope and Frequency

The size, complexity, and level of risk connected with the organization's coding processes will all affect the scope and frequency of internal audits. Audits should generally be performed at least once a year. However, more regular audits are advised for high-risk sectors or in response to particular compliance issues. A representative sample of coded records should be evaluated during audits, with an emphasis on things like:

- ICD, CPT, and HCPCS codes are used for diagnoses and procedures.
- Codes for modifiers and places of service
- Medical justification and supporting documentation for coded services
- Billing and reimbursement procedures, such as how claims are submitted and how rejections or appeals are handled

Audit Process

The internal auditing procedure should be organized and systematic, generally consisting of the following steps:

1. **Planning:** Plan the audit's scope, objectives, methodology, the records to be examined, and the standards for judging coding accuracy.
2. **Data gathering:** To evaluate the correctness and comprehensiveness of coded information and obtain and analyze the necessary paperwork, such as medical records, coding worksheets, and billing statements.
3. **Analysis:** Using the coded data compared to the appropriate coding requirements and accompanying documentation, find and quantify coding mistakes, discrepancies, or potential noncompliance.
4. **Reporting:** Write down the audit findings, including the kinds and numbers of problems found, and give the results to management or the company's compliance committee.
5. **Corrective Action:** Create and carry out a disciplinary action plan to remedy the problems found and stop noncompliance.

Corrective Action Planning

A corrective action plan must be created and put into effect when audit findings point to potential noncompliance, mistakes, or areas for improvement to resolve these problems and reduce the likelihood of disobedience in the future.

Root Cause Analysis

A root cause analysis should be conducted to identify the fundamental causes of the issues raised. This could involve elements like:

- Medical coders need more education or training.
- inadequate control or monitoring of coding procedures
- Documentation requirements or coding guidelines that are unclear or inconsistent
- Systemic problems, such as old or ineffective rules and regulations

Corrective Action Strategies

Organizations should create focused strategies to resolve the issues found and stop future noncompliance based on the root cause analysis. These tactics could consist of the following:

- Providing medical coders and other personnel engaged in the coding process with additional training or education
- Clarifying or updating coding standards and guidelines
- Putting new resources or technologies into practice to increase coding efficiency and accuracy, such as software or reference materials
- Enhancing oversight and control of coding procedures, including the implementation of regular quality assurance or peer review procedures

- To ensure accurate and thorough documentation, medical coders, doctors, and other healthcare workers should work together and communicate better.

Monitoring and Evaluation

Once remedial measures have been implemented, monitoring their efficacy and assessing how they affect coding accuracy and compliance is crucial. Evaluate the changes in coding procedures and pinpoint any persistent or fresh areas of concern; this may entail carrying out follow-up audits or reviews. A mechanism for monitoring and reporting on compliance efforts, including the implementation of corrective actions and their results, should be established by organizations.

Medical coders and healthcare organizations must implement a thorough compliance program to maintain compliance with federal and state requirements, reduce the risk of noncompliance, and ensure the correct and ethical coding of health information. Organizations can promote a culture of compliance and contribute to the overall integrity of the healthcare system by developing solid rules and procedures, offering ongoing education and training, performing regular internal audits, and implementing targeted corrective action plans.

Medical coders are essential in assuring the highest levels of patient care, reimbursement accuracy, and regulatory conformance by remaining abreast of industry changes, upholding a commitment to ethical coding procedures, and actively participating in compliance processes.

Key Takeaways

In conclusion, the essential elements of an effective compliance program for medical coding are as follows:

- Creating and implementing specific policies and processes that set moral and accurate coding standards.
- Creating a code of conduct outlines expectations for appropriate behavior and highlights the organization's dedication to compliance.
- Medical coders and other staff members participating in the coding process should receive continual education and training to ensure their knowledge and abilities are current with industry standards and legal regulations.
- Internal audits are regularly carried out to evaluate coding accuracy, pinpoint areas for improvement, and lower the risk of noncompliance.
- Putting into practice corrective action plans in response to audit findings, dealing with underlying issues, and stopping future non-compliance.
- Maintaining the highest standards of coding accuracy and regulatory conformance by monitoring, assessing, and improving the compliance program as necessary.

Keeping these standards and actively participating in the compliance process can contribute to the effectiveness of the healthcare system and the overall quality of patient care.

TOOLS AND TECHNOLOGY

The medical coding field has significantly evolved with advancements in tools and technology that improve accuracy, efficiency, and consistency. This chapter will explore the essential tools and technologies used in medical coding, including coding manuals, software solutions, Electronic Health Records (EHRs), and various online resources.

Coding Manuals

Medical coding is built on coding guides, which offer a standardized system for categorizing diagnoses, treatments, and services. Medical coders use three main code sets:

- **ICD-10-CM:** In all healthcare settings, diagnoses are reported using the International Classification of Diseases, 10th Revision, Clinical Modification (ICD-10-CM).
- **CPT:** Procedures and services rendered by medical professionals are reported using the Current Procedural Terminology (CPT) code system.
- **HCPCS:** Medical devices, supplies, and non-physician services are reported using the Healthcare Common Procedure Coding System (HCPCS).

Medical Coding Software

Software for medical coding has evolved into a crucial tool for coders, including features that simplify and enhance accuracy. Key characteristics include:

- Look up a code quickly to find its description or a specific code.
- Code verification: Look for possible mistakes or discrepancies in the chosen codes.
- Crosswalks for coding: Map codes between several classification schemes.
- Get updates when code sets are altered automatically.

Options for standard medical coding software include:

- 3M Codefinder
- Optum360 Encoder
- EncoderPro

Electronic Health Records (EHRs)

The way EHRs have changed healthcare professionals record and share patient information. To evaluate clinical paperwork, gather pertinent data, and assign the proper codes, medical coders can use EHRs. EHRs have several benefits:

- **Better access:** Coders now have remote access to patient records, which allows for more adaptability and teamwork.
- **Improved documentation:** EHRs frequently come with built-in templates that help doctors record correct and comprehensive information.
- **Error reduction:** Transcriptional errors and illegible handwriting can be avoided with EHRs.

Online Resources

Medical coders can find help from several internet resources for their regular work and continuous education:

- **Coding guidelines:** Official ICD-10-CM, CPT, and HCPCS coding rules are posted online, giving coders access to the most recent data.
- Resources from the Centers for Medicare & Medicaid Services (CMS): The CMS provides a variety of coding, billing, and reimbursement-related information.
- **NCCI revisions:** To help avoid incorrect coding and billing, the National Correct Coding Initiative (NCCI) keeps a database of coding edits.
- **Organizations for professionals:** Webinars, papers, and forums are among the helpful resources offered by groups like AHIMA and AAPC.

Computer-Assisted Coding (CAC)

Computer-Assisted Coding (CAC) systems use Natural Language Processing (NLP) technology to assess clinical documentation and make code suggestions. CAC can provide several advantages, but more is needed to replace human coders.

- **Efficiency gain:** CAC helps hasten the coding process by automating the initial code selection.
- **Increased consistency:** CAC can ensure that similar cases are coded similarly throughout the organization.
- **Improved accuracy:** CAC can assist in identifying potential coding mistakes or oversights by suggesting codes based on clinical documentation.

Mobile Apps

Many mobile apps have been created to assist medical coders, providing easy access to coding information, tools, and educational materials. Popular medical coding apps include, for instance:

1. ICD-10 Virtual Code Book
2. CPT QuickRef
3. HCPCS Lookup

Integrated Billing and Coding Systems

Medical coding, claim submission, and payment monitoring features are all combined in integrated billing and coding systems, which many healthcare companies use. These technologies can increase communication between coders and billing employees, streamline procedures, and lessen the possibility of billing mistakes. Some standard integrated systems are:

1. Kareo
2. NextGen Healthcare
3. eClinicalWorks

Telecommuting and Remote Coding Technologies

Thanks to technological advancements, medical coders can now work remotely, view patient records, and communicate with coworkers from any location. Remote coding tools, like private virtual networks (VPNs) for security and cloud-based EHRs, let coders work effectively and safely from their homes or other off-site locations.

Data Analytics Tools

Medical coders and healthcare organizations can use data analytics technologies to spot patterns, track performance, and streamline procedures. Organizations can learn more by examining coded data in areas like:

1. Coding productivity and accuracy
2. Denial rates and reasons
3. Revenue trends and reimbursement patterns
4. Clinical documentation improvement opportunities

Popular data analytics tools used in healthcare include:

1. Tableau
2. Microsoft Power BI
3. Qlik Sense

Training and Education Technologies

Coders must keep up with developments in the business and update their abilities as the medical coding sector develops. Access to education and training resources for coders, frequently from the comfort of their homes, has been made possible by technologies like online learning platforms, webinars, and virtual conferences. Online learning platforms include, for instance:

1. AAPC online courses
2. AHIMA virtual learning environment
3. Coursera and Udemy healthcare courses

Utilizing tools and technology is essential for preserving accuracy, efficiency, and compliance as medical coding develops. Medical coders can expedite their everyday activities, improve their skills, and keep up with changes in the field by utilizing these technologies. Incorporating technology into medical coding processes will stay a crucial component of upholding the highest standards of patient care, reimbursement accuracy, and regulatory conformance as the healthcare landscape changes.

Data management software

For healthcare businesses to handle, store, and analyze the enormous amounts of data produced by medical coding systems, data management software is a need. The numerous data management software options used in medical coding will be examined in this chapter, with an emphasis on their features, advantages, and uses.

Practice Management Systems (PMS)

Practice management systems (PMS) are intended to handle administrative duties including scheduling appointments, billing, and claims management. They frequently contain data management features for medical coding specialists. PMS's primary attributes include:

1. Data archiving and retrieval: PMS systems archive coded data and make it readily available for reporting and analysis.
2. Reports capabilities: Create personalized reports to track coding trends, payment habits, and other important performance factors (KPIs).
3. Connectivity with EHRs: PMS applications frequently offer easy data sharing through integration with EHR systems.

Notable PMS software solutions are:

- Kareo
- AdvancedMD
- Athenahealth

Cloud-Based Data Management Solutions

Cloud-based data management solutions provide a scalable and adaptable replacement for conventional on-premise software systems. The following are the advantages of cloud-based solutions for managing medical coding data:

1. Scalability: Cloud-based systems may grow or shrink to meet shifting data processing and storage requirements.
2. Accessibility: Data is available online and accessible from any location with an internet connection, allowing for remote work and collaboration.
3. Security and compliance: Cloud-based systems frequently provide strong security safeguards and integrated compliance capabilities, such as audit trails and access controls, to ensure compliance.

Examples of cloud-based data management solutions include:

- Amazon Web Services (AWS)
- Microsoft Azure
- Google Cloud Platform

Specialized Medical Coding Data Management Software

Specific software solutions are designed to store, arrange, and analyze coded data in a predetermined manner with medical coding data management in mind. Essential components include the following:

- **Tailored data organization:** Arrange and store coded information according to the specifications of a medical facility.
- **Comprehensive search functions:** Locate and obtain particular codes or records with ease.
- **Monitoring coding techniques** is one way to ensure that regulations and industry standards are followed.

Specialized medical coding data management software examples are as follows:
- Medforce
- HealthDox
- Compliance 360

Solutions for Data Backup and Recovery

Efficient data backup and recovery solutions are necessary to safeguard coded data from loss, corruption, or unauthorized access. These choices provide:

- **Regular data backups:** Coded data should be automatically backed up at predefined intervals to lower the risk of data loss.
- **Data encryption:** Protecting confidential patient information and coding data with encryption technology.
- **Disaster recovery:** Offer efficient and timely data recovery during system failures, hacks, or other emergencies.

Typical healthcare data backup and recovery options include:
- Acronis
- Datto
- Veeam

Tools for Cooperation and Communication

Effective communication and teamwork are essential for medical coding teams, especially remotely. Collaboration and communication tools can enhance data management practices in the following ways:
- **Facilitating instantaneous communication:** Coders, auditors, and other team members can communicate via instant messaging, video conferencing, and screen sharing.
- **Streamlining the exchange of documents:** Assign code guides, instructions, and other materials to team members.
- **Promoting knowledge sharing:** Establish a common repository for business news, teaching materials, and code writing rules.

The following are some instances of cooperation and communication methods utilized in medical coding:
- Microsoft Teams
- Zoom
- Slack

Medical coders must manage their data well to maintain compliance, efficiency, and accuracy. Healthcare organizations can use a range of data management software alternatives to improve coding practices, assess performance, and optimize workflows. As the medical coding business grows, using state-of-the-art data management systems will remain critical to guaranteeing the highest standards of patient care, payment accuracy, and regulatory compliance.

Automation tools

Medical coding can be revolutionized by automation technologies that increase accuracy, expedite processes, and reduce time spent on manual tasks. This section will go over the several automation technologies used in medical coding in detail, as well as their benefits and applications.

Optical Character Recognition (OCR) Tools

OCR software transforms text from scanned documents or photos into digital text that can be read by computers. OCR tools can help with the following when it comes to medical coding:

1. Information extraction: From paper records, automatically extract patient demographics, diagnoses, and treatments.
2. A decrease in manual entry reduces the amount of human data entry required, saving time and minimizing errors.
3. Create digital records from paper documents for integration with EHRs or coding applications.

Popular OCR tools include:

- ABBYY FineReader
- Adobe Acrobat Pro DC
- Tesseract

Natural Language Processing (NLP) Solutions

NLP technology enables computers to understand, interpret, and generate human language. In medical coding, NLP solutions can:

1. Code suggestion: Analyze clinical documentation to identify relevant terms and suggest appropriate codes.
2. Terminology mapping: Automatically map clinical terms to standardized coding systems.
3. Quality control: Identify potential coding errors, inconsistencies, or missing information.

Examples of NLP solutions for medical coding include:

- Linguamatics
- Apixio
- Clinithink

Robotic Process Automation (RPA)

RPA technology uses software robots to automate repetitive, rule-based tasks. RPA can be applied to medical coding processes such as:

1. Data entry: Automate the input of patient information, codes, and other data into billing systems or EHRs.
2. Data validation: Automatically cross-check codes against coding guidelines and payer-specific rules.
3. Claim submission: Automate the generation and submission of electronic claims to insurance companies.

RPA tools often used in healthcare include:

- UiPath
- Blue Prism
- Automation Anywhere

Machine Learning (ML) Algorithms

ML algorithms learn from data and make predictions or decisions based on that information. In medical coding, ML algorithms can be used for:

1. Predictive analytics: Forecast trends, such as denial rates, based on historical data.
2. Anomaly detection: Identify unusual patterns or outliers in coded data, potentially indicating errors or fraud.
3. Code optimization: Suggest the most appropriate codes based on provider-specific patterns and historical data.

Examples of ML tools and frameworks include:

- TensorFlow
- Scikit-learn
- H2O.ai

Workflow Automation Software

Workflow automation software helps to streamline and automate complex processes, such as medical coding and billing workflows. These tools can:

1. Task automation: Automate repetitive tasks, such as data entry or code validation.
2. Process standardization: Enforce consistent workflows and processes across the organization.
3. Performance monitoring: Track the progress of tasks and workflows in real-time.

Popular workflow automation software options include:
- Nintex
- Kissflow
- Process Street

Speech Recognition Technology

Speech recognition technology converts spoken language into written text. In medical coding, speech recognition can be utilized in the following ways:

1. Dictation support: Allow providers to dictate clinical documentation directly into EHRs, reducing transcription costs and delays.
2. Coding assistance: Analyze spoken language to suggest potential codes during the coding process.
3. Voice command integration: Enable hands-free navigation and command execution within coding software or EHRs.

Speech recognition tools used in healthcare include:

- Nuance Dragon Medical
- M*Modal Fluency Direct
- Google Cloud Speech-to-Text

Artificial Intelligence (AI) Platforms

AI platforms combine machine learning, natural language processing, and other advanced technologies to facilitate automation and enhance decision-making in medical coding. AI platforms can be employed for:

1. Intelligent code suggestion: Analyze clinical documentation and provide accurate code suggestions based on context.
2. Automated audits: Conduct automatic audits to identify coding errors, inconsistencies, or areas for improvement.
3. Continuous learning: Adapt and improve coding recommendations over time as the system learns from user interactions and feedback.

Examples of AI platforms for medical coding include:

- IBM Watson Health
- Google Cloud Healthcare API
- Amazon Comprehend Medical

Interoperability and Integration Tools

Interoperability and integration tools facilitate data exchange and communication between various healthcare systems, such as EHRs, billing software, and medical coding tools. These tools can enhance medical coding processes by:

1. Streamlining data transfer: Automate the flow of data between systems, reducing manual intervention and potential errors.
2. Standardizing data formats: Convert data into standardized formats for seamless integration and analysis.
3. Enabling real-time data access: Provide up-to-date patient information and coding data across systems for accurate and timely decision-making.

Examples of interoperability and integration tools include:

- Redox
- Health Level Seven (HL7) Standards
- Fast Healthcare Interoperability Resources (FHIR)

Automation tools have the potential to revolutionize medical coding by improving accuracy, efficiency, and compliance. By leveraging these cutting-edge tools, medical coding professionals can spend less time on manual tasks and focus on higher-level decision-making and analysis. As the healthcare landscape continues to evolve, embracing automation technologies will remain a vital aspect of maintaining the highest standards of patient care, reimbursement accuracy, and regulatory adherence.

CAREER ADVICE

We welcome you to the career guidance chapter of our comprehensive book, Medical Coding. This chapter intends to give you crucial knowledge and useful advice for beginning a prosperous career in medical coding, a field constantly expanding in the American healthcare sector.

The need for knowledgeable medical coders grows as the healthcare system develops and expands. Medical coders are essential to healthcare reimbursement because they convert diagnoses, equipment, and medical procedures into standardized codes that guarantee accurate billing and prompt payment. In addition to streamlining the financial aspects of healthcare, this enhances the general effectiveness and standard of patient treatment.

This chapter will examine the numerous facets of developing a lucrative medical coding profession. The educational and professional credentials required to stand out in this cutthroat area will be covered first. The American Academy of Professional Coders (AAPC) and the American Health Information Management Association (AHIMA), commonly regarded as the gold standard in medical coding certification, will be discussed in detail, along with their major certifications.

We will then examine the various work environments and career options for medical coders. Whether you want to work for a big hospital, a small private practice, or even remotely from the comfort of your home, we can help you find and land the job that most closely matches your objectives, personally and professionally.

We will advise on acquiring the knowledge and abilities that companies look for most in medical coders to help you succeed in your chosen field. This encompasses hard skills like coding expertise and technical understanding and soft skills like communication, critical thinking, and attention to detail. We will also offer guidance on keeping up with the rapidly evolving medical coding environment, including remaining current with market developments and regulatory changes.

A successful career in this cutthroat industry requires networking and professional development, which we will cover in detail. We will introduce you to important tools like online discussion boards, trade shows, and regional AAPC and AHIMA chapters that help you network with other professionals and keep up with the most recent advancements in medical coding.

We will go through potential career routes and the competencies required to succeed in these positions for those who aspire to leadership roles within the medical coding community. We will offer advice on how to set yourself up for success in these professions, whether your goal is to work as a coding manager, consultant, or educator.

The final section will discuss the importance of work-life balance and self-care for medical coders. For your general well-being and job happiness, building healthy habits and coping mechanisms is imperative, as working as a programmer may put you under high pressure and short deadlines.

This chapter will provide case studies, anecdotes, and observations from seasoned medical coders who have successfully navigated the difficulties and rewards of this fast-paced industry. Our objective is to arm you with the information and resources required to establish a fruitful career in medical coding by offering helpful advice, doable tactics, and worthwhile resources.

When you begin this thrilling journey, remember that your commitment, diligence, and enthusiasm for the subject will be your greatest strengths. We cordially encourage you to explore this chapter and learn the medical coding industry's top secrets for success. Welcome aboard, and best wishes for a successful career!

Some career advices

We want to give you some general career guidance that you can use at different points in your medical coding career. You can use the advice in this article to make wise choices, reach your full potential, and succeed in your chosen area over the long run.

1. Have definite career objectives: Have a clear idea of what you want your career in medical coding to include. This will direct you in selecting the appropriate career prospects and work environments and assist you in making smart decisions regarding your education, certification, and professional growth.
2. Invest in your education by finishing an accredited medical coding program and earning the necessary certifications. Your knowledge and abilities will grow, making you more marketable for jobs.
3. Create a strong professional network: Professional networking is essential for advancing one's career. To network with colleagues, mentors, and prospective employers, participate in online forums, attend industry events, and join professional organizations. Throughout your career, these contacts can offer you, helpful counsel, leads on jobs, and assistance.
4. Accept lifelong learning: Keep up with the latest coding standards, legal updates, and market trends. Maintain your expertise and remain flexible in the always-changing world of medical coding by regularly updating your skills and knowledge through workshops, webinars, and online courses.
5. Develop your soft skills: While technical expertise is essential, soft skills like communication, teamwork, and problem-solving can help you stand out from the competition and advance your career. To advance your professional development, actively work on developing these abilities.
6. Highlight your accomplishments by keeping an up-to-date CV and LinkedIn page emphasizing your training, credentials, abilities, and successes. It will be simpler for prospective employers to see your value as a medical coder, and it will help you stand out to them.
7. Be proactive in your job search: Look for openings on job boards, connect with people in your network, and go to career fairs rather than waiting for them to come to you. Create a CV and cover letter for each job you're applying for, highlighting your most valuable qualifications.

8. To be prepared for interviews:

   - Thoroughly investigate potential companies.
   - Be ready to discuss your abilities, prior experiences, and desired career path.
   - Consider how you can convince potential employers of your worth as a medical coder as you practice responding to typical interview questions.

9. Seek mentorship and guidance: List seasoned individuals who can provide direction, counsel, and support as you progress as a medical coder. A mentor may offer priceless advice, direct you away from frequent traps, and encourage you when things become tough.

10. To maintain a healthy work-life balance, draw boundaries between your personal and professional lives and give yourself a priority. By doing this, you can avoid burnout and maintain your physical and emotional well-being. As a medical coder, this will support your ability to stay interested, productive, and focused.

By incorporating these career counseling suggestions into your professional journey, you can create the foundation for a fulfilling and profitable career in medical coding. While you learn and advance in this dynamic industry, remember to be flexible and dedicated and accept new challenges enthusiastically and passionately.

Required Skills and Competencies

Medical coding is a highly specialized subject that calls for a certain set of abilities. To succeed in this field, aspiring medical coders need a solid foundation in several areas, including medical language, coding systems, regulatory compliance, and soft skills. We will give a thorough review of the fundamental abilities and knowledge necessary for a successful career in medical coding in this part.

Medical Terminology and Anatomy

Medical coders must have a thorough knowledge of human anatomy and medical jargon. Thanks to this understanding, coders can effectively evaluate clinical data and assign the proper codes for diagnoses, procedures, and services. Priority regions include:

- **Basic medical jargon:** To correctly decode medical records, medical coders must be proficient in the language of healthcare, including common prefixes, suffixes, and root terms.
- **Anatomy and physiology:** Understanding the anatomy and physiology of the human body is crucial for comprehending medical procedures and conditions. Major body systems, organs, tissues, and prevalent illnesses and disorders should be known to coders.
- **Pathology:** To correctly code diagnoses, medical coders must have a fundamental understanding of disease processes, including kinds, causes, and consequences on the body.

- **Pharmacology:** To properly code medication-related services and operations, one must be knowledgeable about generic pharmaceuticals, drug classifications, and their therapeutic purposes.

Coding Systems and Guidelines

Medical coders must be skilled in various coding systems, each with rules and norms. Systems for key coding include:

- The World Health Organization's International Classification of Diseases (ICD) system categorizes diagnoses and external sources of injuries. Medical coders must be knowledgeable about the most recent ICD and any revisions and modifications to the classification scheme.
- The American Medical Association created the Current Procedural Terminology (CPT) system, used to code medical operations and services given by doctors and other healthcare workers. Medical coders must know about CPT recommendations, modifiers, and appropriate code selection.
- Medical services, treatments, and equipment not covered by the CPT system are denoted by HCPCS codes, which stand for Healthcare Common Procedure Coding System. Medical coders must be familiar with the various HCPCS code levels and their proper application because these codes are generally utilized for Medicare and Medicaid billing.
- Diagnosis-Related Group (DRG): DRGs classify patients based on their diagnoses, procedures, and other characteristics and are used for inpatient hospital billing. Medical coders should understand the DRG categorization system and the associated rules for allocating DRG codes.

Regulatory Compliance and Reimbursement

Medical coders are essential in ensuring that healthcare practitioners are paid fairly for their services. To do this, coders must comprehend the intricate network of laws and policies that govern healthcare billing, such as:

- **Federal and state laws:** Medical coders need to be familiar with the laws that affect healthcare reimbursement, including the False Claims Act, the Health Insurance Portability and Accountability Act (HIPAA), and state-specific billing laws.
- **Specific rules for payers:** Each insurance payer has specifications for filing claims and receiving payment. Medical coders need to know the regulations of different payers, such as Medicare, Medicaid, and private insurance firms.
- **Compliance and ethics:** Medical coders preserve the accuracy and integrity of healthcare billing and ensure that all coding and documentation procedures comply with legal and ethical criteria. This entails being watchful for dishonest actions like upcoding, unbundling, and duplicate billing.

Medical coders must be skilled in auditing and quality control procedures to spot and fix coding errors, inconsistencies, and potential compliance problems.

Health Information Management (HIM) and Electronic Health Records (EHR)

Medical coders frequently interact extensively with these records to retrieve the data required for coding. Therefore a firm grasp of HIM principles and EHR systems is crucial. Priority regions include:

- Medical coders should be familiar with the fundamentals of health information management (HIM), including data collection, storage, retrieval, and analysis, and preserving patient confidentiality, privacy, and security.
- Electronic health records: As EHR systems progressively replace paper-based clinical documentation, medical coders must be proficient in their use. Coders should be able to easily navigate and extract the necessary data for coding and be familiar with the structure and functionality of different EHR systems.

Soft Skills and Professional Competencies

Medical coders need a variety of soft skills and professional competencies to succeed in their professions, in addition to technical proficiency. Among the most crucial abilities are the following:

- Pay close attention to the details: Medical coding demands high precision and accuracy because even small mistakes can have a big impact on costs and compliance. Medical coders must be careful and detail-oriented in their work to ensure that codes are allocated accurately and that all pertinent information is recorded.
- Analytical and critical thinking skills: Medical coders must be able to evaluate intricate medical records, find pertinent data, and make defensible choices following coding standards and regulations. Strong critical thinking and problem-solving abilities are needed for this.
- Adaptability: The medical coding industry is always changing due to new laws, code upgrades, and market trends. Medical coders need to be flexible and quick to respond to changes in their workplace.
- Medical coders sometimes operate under strict deadlines and must perform many duties simultaneously. One needs strong time management and organizing skills to handle these expectations and sustain productivity.
- Although medical coding is largely behind-the-scenes, coders must communicate well with coworkers, doctors, and other healthcare professionals to explain documents, settle disagreements, and guarantee accurate coding. Strong verbal and written communication abilities and the capacity for teamwork and collaboration are necessary for this.
- Medical coders may work individually or remotely. Therefore they need a high degree of self-motivation and discipline to remain concentrated and finish duties quickly.

Continuing Education and Professional Development

Medical coders should actively participate in chances for professional development and continuing education to retain their knowledge and stay up to date with developments in the business. This might comprise:

Obtaining advanced certifications: Many medical coders opt to get certified in inpatient coding, outpatient coding, risk adjustment, or medical auditing. These advanced certifications can improve a coder's abilities, boost their marketability, and open up prospects for higher-paying employment.

Regularly attending conferences, seminars, and webinars can help medical coders stay current on the most recent coding improvements, legislative changes, and market trends. Several professional associations, including AAPC and AHIMA, provide webinars, workshops, and seminars on various coding-related subjects.

Participating in online learning: For medical coders, online courses and training modules are a practical and flexible option to advance their knowledge and abilities. Online courses on certain coding systems, regulatory compliance, and other pertinent topics are available from numerous respected businesses and educational institutions.

Accessing industry resources and publications: Medical coders should constantly read blogs, newsletters, and industry publications to stay informed. They can do this to be informed on the most recent information, industry best practices, and expert viewpoints.

Joining professional organizations and local chapters can have several advantages, such as access to educational materials, networking opportunities, and support from professionals who share your interests. Meetings, workshops, and other events that promote career development and connections within the medical coding community are frequently held by local chapters.

Regulatory compliance, interpersonal abilities, medical terminology, and coding systems are among the qualities and skills required for a successful career in medical coding. Aspiring medical coders may set themselves up for long-term success in this fascinating and satisfying career by being versed in these subjects and actively engaging in continuing education and professional development.

Specialization Opportunities for Medical Coders

Medical coders have the chance to specialize in various sub-niches of the healthcare business as it continues to grow and diversify. Because of their ability to specialize, coders can attend to the particular requirements of particular patient populations or healthcare environments. Medical coders can improve their career chances, boost their earning potential, and gain an employment market advantage by pursuing a specialization. This section will discuss various specialization options for medical coders, outlining the peculiar features, prerequisites, and potential advantages of each.

Inpatient Coding

Inpatient coding is the area of medicine that focuses on coding services given to patients admitted to hospitals and other acute care institutions. Complex medical diagnoses, treatments, and procedures while a patient is hospitalized must be given codes by inpatient coders. The Diagnosis-Related Group (DRG) system and the International Classification of Diseases, 10th Revision, Procedure Coding System (ICD-10-PCS), which influence payment rates for inpatient care, must be understood by them.

Medical coders need to thoroughly understand anatomy, physiology, and medical terminology to thrive in inpatient coding. They should also be well-versed in the complexities of hospital billing and coding and the laws and guidelines governing inpatient care. Several certifications are available for those interested in inpatient coding, including the Certified Inpatient Coder (CIC) from the AAPC and the Certified Coding Specialist (CCS) from AHIMA.

Outpatient Coding

Outpatient coding is the process of medically classifying services given to patients who are not admitted to a hospital or other inpatient facility. Outpatient coders code the services rendered in doctor's offices, diagnostic imaging centers, and ambulatory surgery centers. Mostly, they code services, procedures, and supplies using Healthcare Common Procedure Coding System (HCPCS), and Current Procedural Terminology (CPT).

If medical coders wish to specialize in outpatient coding, they must understand the ins and outs of different outpatient healthcare environments and outpatient billing and coding standards. Coders can demonstrate their expertise in outpatient coding by obtaining certifications such as the Certified Outpatient Coder (COC) from the AAPC or the Certified Coding Specialist - Physician-based (CCS-P) from AHIMA.

Risk Adjustment Coding

To determine the appropriate payment rates for healthcare providers, a specific kind of medical coding known as risk adjustment coding focuses on precisely capturing the severity and complexity of a patient's medical issues; risk adjustment coders primarily utilize the International Classification of Diseases, 10th Revision, Clinical Modification (ICD-10-CM) to assign diagnostic codes that accurately reflect a patient's health status. They are crucial to ensuring fair pay for medical professionals, particularly those who care for patients with numerous chronic illnesses or comorbidities.

Coders interested in risk adjustment coding should familiarize themselves with the Hierarchical Condition Category (HCC) model and other risk adjustment models used by public and private payers in addition to the ICD-10-CM. The AAPC offers the Certified Risk Adjustment Coder (CRC) certification to show that a coder is skilled in this area.

Specialty Coding

The medical categorization of treatments, procedures, and diagnoses unique to a given medical specialization or subspecialty is known as specialty coding.

Specialty coding regions include, for instance:

- Cardiology
- Gastroenterology
- Obstetrics and Gynecology
- Oncology
- Orthopedics
- Pediatrics
- Radiology

Specialty coders must be highly knowledgeable about the medical jargon, protocols, and diagnostic standards specific to their specialization. They also need to understand each specialization's unique reimbursement procedures and coding requirements. Specialty coders must keep up with the newest methods, tools, and therapies available as long as medical breakthroughs keep coming.

Medical coders should look for appropriate educational and training alternatives to pursue a career in specialist coding, such as online courses, webinars, and workshops focusing on specialty coding. Specialty-specific coding certificates are provided by numerous professional associations, such as the AAPC and AHIMA, to show that a person is knowledgeable in a particular field. Among the instances are:

1. Certified Cardiology Coder (CCC)
2. Certified Gastroenterology Coder (CGC)
3. Certified Obstetrics and Gynecology Coder (COGC)
4. Certified Oncology Coder (COC)
5. Certified Orthopedic Surgery Coder (COSC)
6. Certified Pediatrics Coder (CPC)
7. Certified Radiology Coder (CRCR)

Coding Auditing

Medical coding auditing is a specialist field that aims to guarantee coding procedures' precision, compliance, and caliber. Coding auditors examine medical data, examine coding patterns, and spot inconsistencies or mistakes that can result in inaccurate billing, inadequate compensation, or even legal problems. They may also offer coding staff feedback, training, and direction to enhance overall coding accuracy and compliance.

Medical coders should have a good experience in medical coding and a comprehensive awareness of coding guidelines, laws, and payer policies to thrive in coding auditing. They must also have exceptional analytical, communication, and problem-solving abilities. Coders who are interested in auditing can pursue certifications that include auditing components in their curricula, such as the Certified Professional Medical Auditor (CPMA) offered by the AAPC or the Certified Coding Specialist (CCS) or Certified Coding Specialist - Physician-based (CCS-P) offered by AHIMA.

Coding Education and Training

Medical coders with a strong desire to coach and teach others can consider specializing in coding instruction and training. Medical coders who are just starting or have some experience might benefit from the educational resources, workshops, and training courses that coding educators create and provide. They could be employed in various places, such as academic institutions, healthcare facilities, or professional associations.

Medical coders should have extensive medical coding experience and great presentation, communication, and interpersonal skills if they want to become coding educators. Having the appropriate teaching or instructional design credentials may also benefit them. The AAPC provides the Certified Professional Coding Instructor (CPC-I) certification for those considering a career in coding teaching. Finally, specialization options in medical coding offer a wide range of chances for coders seeking to enhance their careers, broaden their skill set, and have a bigger impact on the healthcare sector.

Medical coders can differentiate themselves from competitors, boost their earning potential, and gain access to new, exciting career prospects by pursuing a specialization. The American Academy of Professional Coders (AAPC) offers specialty-specific coding certifications to certify a medical coder's proficiency in a particular field. These credentials prove a coder's expertise in the particular coding standards, practices, and diagnostic requirements connected to each medical specialty. The stated specialty coding certifications are summarized below:

Certified Cardiology Coder (CCC)

The CCC certification focuses on the medical coding of cardiology procedures, diagnoses, and services. Cardiology coders must be familiar with the intricacies of cardiovascular anatomy, terminology, and the procedures involved in diagnosing and treating heart-related conditions. The CCC examination tests a coder's knowledge of CPT, ICD-10-CM, and HCPCS coding for various cardiology services, such as cardiac catheterization, electrophysiology studies, and echocardiography.

Certified Gastroenterology Coder (CGC)

Medical coders specializing in gastrointestinal diagnoses, operations, and services are eligible for the CGC certification. Gastroenterology coders must know the anatomy and therapeutic techniques used to treat gastrointestinal diseases. Coders take the CGC exam to demonstrate their skill in coding services such as colonoscopies, endoscopies, and hepatobiliary operations according to CPT, ICD-10-CM, and HCPCS.

Certified Obstetrics and Gynecology Coder (COGC)

The COGC certification focuses on the medical coding of obstetrics and gynecology procedures, diagnoses, and services. Obstetrics and gynecology coders must be well-versed in the female reproductive system's anatomy and the various procedures and treatments associated with women's health. The COGC examination tests a coder's knowledge of CPT, ICD-10-CM, and HCPCS coding for services such as prenatal care, delivery, and gynecological surgeries.

Certified Oncology Coder (COC)

The COC certification is designed for medical coders specializing in coding oncology procedures, diagnoses, and services. Oncology coders must understand cancer-related terminology, staging, and the various diagnostic and therapeutic procedures used to treat cancer. The COC examination assesses a coder's proficiency in CPT, ICD-10-CM, and HCPCS coding for services such as chemotherapy administration, radiation therapy, and cancer surgery.

Certified Orthopedic Surgery Coder (COSC)

The COSC certification focuses on the medical coding of orthopedic surgery procedures, diagnoses, and services. Orthopedic surgery coders must be familiar with the anatomy of the musculoskeletal system and the various surgical procedures used to treat orthopedic conditions. The COSC examination tests a coder's knowledge of CPT, ICD-10-CM, and HCPCS coding for services such as joint replacements, spinal surgeries, and fracture treatments.

Certified Pediatrics Coder (CPC)

The CPC certification is designed for medical coders who specialize in coding pediatric procedures, diagnoses, and services. Pediatric coders must comprehensively understand the unique medical terminology, growth and development milestones, and diagnostic and treatment procedures specific to pediatric patients. The CPC examination assesses a coder's proficiency in CPT, ICD-10-CM, and HCPCS coding for services such as well-child exams, immunizations, and pediatric surgeries.

Certified Radiology Coder (CRCR)

The CRCR certification focuses on the medical coding of radiology procedures, diagnoses, and services. Radiology coders must be well-versed in anatomy, medical terminology, and the various diagnostic and therapeutic imaging procedures used in radiology, such as X-rays, MRI, and CT scans. The CRCR examination tests a coder's knowledge of CPT, ICD-10-CM, and HCPCS coding for services such as diagnostic imaging, interventional radiology, and nuclear medicine.

To prepare for these specialty-specific certification exams, medical coders should complete relevant training courses, workshops, or webinars focused on the respective medical specialties. These educational resources will help coders develop the necessary knowledge and skills to excel in their chosen specialty and pass the certification exam. Additionally, some certifications may require a certain amount of professional coding experience in the specialty area or the completion of prerequisite certifications, such as the Certified Professional Coder (CPC) credential, before attempting the specialty exam.

Medical coders who attain specialty coding certification may enjoy several benefits, including greater earning potential, more job prospects, and recognition as experts in their field. Employers often perceive that certified coders are more competent and dedicated to their profession, making them more desirable candidates for positions with higher responsibilities and wages.
Coders can also stay updated with the latest developments and trends by specializing in a particular area of medical coding, ensuring they remain knowledgeable and relevant in an ever-evolving healthcare environment.

Successful Career Paths for Medical Coding

Medical coding is still a vital component of administrative tasks in the constantly changing world of healthcare. As a medical coder, you play a crucial part in converting clinical documentation into generally accepted codes for billing and insurance purposes. The most lucrative employment options for those interested in a career in medical coding will be covered in this chapter. As a Certified Professional Coder (CPC), you'll give diagnoses, procedures, and services rendered by healthcare providers the appropriate medical codes. The American Academy of Professional Coders (AAPC) accreditation will boost your credibility and open doors to lucrative work prospects in medical facilities, clinics, and private practices.

The American Health Information Management Association (AHIMA) offers the Certified Coding Specialist (CCS) credential for people interested in working in hospitals and inpatient institutions. Professionals in the CCS field are skilled in the PCS and ICD-10-CM coding systems, which enables them to code complex medical cases precisely.

Certified Outpatient Coders (COC) are experts in coding medical services offered at ambulatory care facilities, emergency rooms, and outpatient clinics. COC professionals concentrate on outpatient settings. The AAPC accreditation ensures your ability to manage the nuances of outpatient coding. By assuring the correctness of risk adjustment coding, you will contribute to the financial stability of healthcare organizations as a Certified Risk Adjustment Coder (CRC). As appropriate coding directly affects reimbursement rates, this position is especially crucial for businesses working with Medicare and Medicaid. To prove your proficiency in this niche area, the AAPC offers the CRC certification.

Medical Coding Auditor: If you have experience in medical coding, you could move into an auditing position. Medical coding auditors must evaluate coded medical records to find errors, compliance problems, and possible fraud. Your level of knowledge in this field will be confirmed by earning the Certified Professional Medical Auditor (CPMA) credential from the AAPC.

Medical Coding Educator: If you love to educate, consider exploring working in medical coding. You'll be responsible for educating aspiring programmers, providing continuing education programs, and keeping current with market developments. The Certified Professional Coding Instructor (CPC-I) accreditation from the AAPC might aid in your quest to become known as an industry authority. You will be essential to the healthcare sector by pursuing these lucrative job opportunities in medical coding. Your professional credibility will increase thanks to certification from reputable organizations like the AAPC and AHIMA, which will also open doors to rewarding and lucrative prospects.

Roles

Professional Coder Certified (CPC)

A CPC's major responsibility is to review and evaluate medical records from healthcare providers to assign the proper codes to diagnoses, treatments, and services. They maintain compliance with governmental rules and industry standards while ensuring proper coding for billing and insurance purposes. CPCs operate in various healthcare facilities, including clinics, hospitals, and private offices.

Certified Coding Specialist (CCS)

Role: Coding medical services offered in hospitals and inpatient facilities is the primary responsibility of CCS specialists. They can manage complicated medical cases because of their in-depth understanding of the ICD-10-CM (diagnoses) and ICD-10-PCS (procedures) coding systems. Their main duties are reviewing medical records, assigning precise codes, and assuring adherence to professional standards and legal requirements.

Certified Outpatient Coder (COC)

COC practitioners are experts in coding medical services for outpatient settings, such as outpatient clinics, ambulatory care facilities, and emergency rooms.
In addition to assigning appropriate codes and assuring compliance with industry standards and federal regulations, they are in charge of examining and interpreting medical documentation. They aid healthcare businesses in maintaining precise billing and payment procedures with their outpatient coding knowledge.

Certified Risk Adjustment Coder (CRC)

The role of CRCs is to capture specific diagnoses and diseases that affect a patient's general health state through risk adjustment coding. To ensure correct coding for risk adjustment purposes, they engage with healthcare organizations, particularly those participating in the Medicare and Medicaid programs. Accurate coding directly affects payment rates, helping healthcare companies maintain their financial viability.

Medical Coding Auditor

Medical coding auditors carry out internal and external audits of medical records that have been coded. They examine and evaluate the accuracy of the medical codes, spot problems with compliance, and look for any fraud. Auditors work with coding specialists, healthcare providers, and administrators to ensure that coding procedures comply with industry standards and legal requirements. They also offer feedback, training, and direction to increase coding accuracy and compliance.

Medical Coding Educator

Medical coding educators' roles include

- instructing and training future medical coders,
- providing continuing education programs for working professionals, and
- keeping up with changes in the field.

They create educational materials, run workshops, and give pupils individualized instruction. Educators promote the best practices in medical coding in conjunction with healthcare organizations, academic institutions, and professional organizations, who also support the field's continual development.

PRACTICE TESTS

Practice Test Effective Medical Coding Techniques and Strategies

1. Which coding system requires familiarity for accurate code assignment?
a. Current Procedural Terminology
b. Universal Procedure Protocols
c. Medical Operations Sequence
d. Health Operation Terminology

2. To improve understanding of coding systems and rules, medical coders can:
a. Attend movie theaters regularly
b. Frequently complete coding tasks and case studies
c. Start their medical practice
d. Design their coding system

3. What is crucial for resolving coding discrepancies?
a. Avoiding communication with healthcare providers
b. Reliance solely on electronic health records
c. Open communication with healthcare professionals
d. Following intuition over guidelines

4. In the medical coding process, what plays a significant role in enhancing efficiency?
a. Leveraging video game technology
b. Using coding software and tools
c. Constantly changing coding rules
d. Ignoring electronic health records

5. What should medical coders prioritize to demonstrate advanced expertise?
a. Acquiring as many online badges as possible
b. Purchasing the latest medical equipment
c. Pursuing additional credentials and certifications
d. Shifting to a different profession

6. For effective medical coding, what is the first crucial step?
a. Hiring an assistant
b. Reviewing patient dietary preferences
c. Analyzing patient medical records in-depth
d. Taking long vacations

7. Which platform can provide valuable support and learning opportunities for medical coders?
a. Social media memes
b. Comedy clubs
c. Professional organizations like AAPC and AHIMA
d. Fast-food chains

8. What is NOT a primary method for ensuring coding accuracy and compliance?
a. Regular Participation in fitness exercises
b. Continuous quality improvement
c. Participation in internal and external audits
d. Implementing corrective action plans

9. When seeking clarification or more details from healthcare providers, how should medical coders communicate?
a. With riddles and puzzles
b. Clear and concise communication
c. Using multiple foreign languages at once
d. Through interpretative dance

10. How can medical coders effectively use technology in the coding process?
a. By solely depending on AI without verification
b. Regularly changing their computer systems
c. Becoming proficient in using EHR systems
d. Ignoring updates on emerging technologies

11. Which one is a crucial strategy for improving medical coding techniques?
a. Prioritizing cooking skills
b. familiarity with coding systems and guidelines
c. Moving to different continents regularly
d. Experimenting with codes without validation

12. In which online space can medical coders share their experiences and insights?
a. Online dating forums
b. Thriller movie review sites
c. Online forums and social media groups dedicated to Medical Coding
d. E-commerce product reviews

13. Which of the following is NOT mentioned as a significant tool for medical coders?
a. Electronic health records (EHRs)
b. AI-driven game applications
c. coding software and tools
d. Tools suggesting automated code

14. What should medical coders regularly monitor to assess the effectiveness of coding practices?
a. Stock market trends
b. Weather patterns
c. Coding performance metrics
d. Latest fashion trends

15. For medical coders, understanding medical jargon and acronyms helps in:
a. Making casual conversation at parties
b. Judging beauty pageants
c. Correctly evaluating patient record data
d. Deciphering ancient languages

16. How can medical coders ensure they capture all relevant data during coding?
a. By guessing the information
b. Establishing a systematic procedure for evaluating medical records
c. Only checking the first page of the record
d. Asking their friends for advice

17. Which organization was NOT listed as a resource for professional networking for medical coders?
a. American Medical Association (AMA)
b. American Academy of Professional Coders (AAPC)
c. American Health Information Management Association (AHIMA)
d. International Medical Coders Association (IMCA)

18. Which of the following is NOT a way to understand coding systems better?
a. Using coding guides and online resources
b. Relying solely on personal experience
c. Engaging in ongoing education
d. Completing coding tasks and case studies frequently

19. Which tool offers automated code suggestions to assist in the coding process?
a. Basic calculators
b. Food recipe apps
c. coding software and tools
d. Music streaming platforms

20. Which of the following is a method to ensure all pertinent data is captured during coding?
a. Ignoring doctor's notes and relying only on test results
b. Carefully reviewing every aspect of the medical record
c. Skimming through records quickly
d. Depending on patients to provide Coding information

21. To promote more accurate coding, medical coders should:
a. Avoid discussing documentation with healthcare professionals
b. Only communicate through written letters
c. Discuss options for improving documentation with healthcare professionals
d. Rely solely on their intuition

22. Which strategy involves a combination of in-depth knowledge of coding systems, record analysis, and use of technology?
a. Effective medical coding techniques
b. Basic first aid skills
c. Advanced driving techniques
d. Gardening techniques

23. To stay current with the latest medical coding trends, medical coders should:
a. Avoid all industry events
b. Attend comedy shows
c. Attend industry conferences and events
d. Take a break from the profession

24. How should medical coders approach unclear information in patient records?
a. Guess the meaning
b. Overlook the data
c. Communicate with healthcare professionals for clarification
d. Ask their family members for input

25. What can medical coders use to revolutionize the medical coding process in the future?
a. Novels and fiction books
b. Their dreams and visions
c. Advancements in AI and machine learning technologies
d. Looking into a crystal ball

26. Which activity helps medical coders put their understanding of coding systems into practice?
a. Swimming
b. Completing coding tasks and case studies
c. Painting
d. Hiking

27. What's the purpose of regular coding audits?
a. To create more work for coders
b. To ensure adherence to coding guidelines
c. To entertain the staff
d. As a formality with no real purpose

28. Which of the following is NOT a way to improve documentation quality?
a. Clear communication with healthcare professionals
b. Regular training on documentation best practices
c. Ignoring feedback and suggestions
d. Implementing corrective action plans

29. Where can medical coders get resources to understand evolving coding standards better?
a. Mystery novels
b. Professional organizations like AAPC and AHIMA
c. Children's storybooks
d. Cookbooks

30. What should be a primary goal for medical coders to ensure accurate billing and insurance claims?
a. Efficient party planning
b. Accurate code assignment
c. Doodling in free time
d. Changing coding rules daily

Practice Test Laws and Regulations

1. What year was the Health Insurance Portability and Accountability Act (HIPAA) established?
a) 1986
b) 1990
c) 1996
d) 2002

2. What does the Security Rule of HIPAA primarily concern?
a) Standardized codes
b) Electronic PHI
c) False claims
d) Referrals

3. Which code set does HIPAA NOT mandate to use?
a) ICD
b) CPT
c) HCPCS
d) ABCD

4. The False Claims Act mainly targets:
a) Patient referrals
b) PHI disclosures
c) Fraudulent government claims
d) Medical training

5. What does the Anti-Kickback Statute prevent?
a) Unauthorized PHI disclosure
b) Payments for eligible patient referrals
c) Use of standardized codes
d) Doctor self-referrals

6. Stark Law, also known as the Physician Self-Referral Law, prohibits:
a) Fraudulent government claims
b) Disclosing PHI without authorization
c) Doctors referring Medicare and Medicaid patients to entities they have business relationships with
d) Use of non-standardized codes

7. Who has modified the World Health Organization's (WHO) ICD system for use in the US?
a) AMA
b) WHO
c) CMS and NCHS
d) ABC

8. The CPT coding system was created by which organization?
a) WHO
b) CMS
c) NCHS
d) AMA

9. Which Act, passed in 2010, is also commonly known as Obamacare?
a) Stark Law
b) HIPAA
c) Affordable Care Act (ACA)
d) False Claims Act

10. Which of the following is NOT a primary objective of ACA?
a) Protecting PHI
b) Promoting EHRs
c) Preventing fraud, waste, and abuse
d) Expanding access to health insurance

11. What is the primary focus of the ACA in relation to care?
a) Fee-for-service
b) Value-based care
c) Outpatient care
d) Inpatient care

12. The ACA accelerated the switch from:
a) CPT to HCPCS
b) ICD-9 to ICD-10
c) HIPAA to Stark Law
d) CMS to NCHS

13. Under the HIPAA Privacy Rule, what is typically NOT permitted without patient consent?
a) Disclosure of PHI
b) Use of PHI for treatment
c) Use of PHI for payment
d) Use of PHI for healthcare operations

14. The ACA emphasized the importance of:
a) Manual health records
b) Fee-for-service models
c) Electronic Health Records (EHRs)
d) Standalone healthcare systems

15. Which entity is primarily responsible for overseeing Medicare and Medicaid in the US?
a) WHO
b) AMA
c) CMS
d) NCHS

16. Which Act introduced measures to boost the prevention of fraud, waste, and abuse in healthcare?
a) Stark Law
b) Anti-Kickback Statute
c) Affordable Care Act (ACA)
d) False Claims Act

17. The ACA provided funding for projects aimed at:
a) Promoting fee-for-service models
b) Developing a skilled healthcare workforce
c) Promoting paper-based health records
d) Reverting to ICD-9 coding system

18. Which rule establishes the benchmark for protecting patient medical records and PHI?
a) HIPAA Security Rule
b) ACA Privacy Rule
c) CMS Security Rule
d) HIPAA Privacy Rule

19. Under the ACA, the main shift in focus for care models was from:
a) Inpatient to outpatient
b) Outpatient to inpatient
c) Fee-for-service to value-based
d) Value-based to fee-for-service

20. What is the primary purpose of the National Correct Coding Initiative (NCCI)?
a) Promote electronic health records
b) Ensure proper use of coding procedures
c) Discourage the use of standardized codes
d) Promote fee-for-service models

21. Which organization is housed within the US Department of Health and Human Services (HHS)?
a) WHO
b) AMA
c) CMS
d) NCHS

22. Which coding system offers a higher level of detail and granularity in classification, enabling better patient care tracking?
a) ICD-9
b) ICD-10
c) CPT
d) HCPCS

23. Which of the following does the Stark Law specifically address?
a) Kickbacks for patient referrals
b) Physician self-referrals
c) Fraudulent claims to the government
d) Disclosure of PHI

24 . Who is responsible for the creation of the Current Procedural Terminology (CPT) coding system?
a) CMS
b) NCHS
c) AMA
d) WHO

25. The ACA promotes what type of healthcare model?
a) Fee-for-service
b) Value-based care
c) Inpatient care
d) Outpatient care

26. What type of entities does the Stark Law concern with in terms of referrals?
a) Government-owned entities
b) Private hospitals
c) Entities physicians have financial relationships with
d) Overseas healthcare entities

27. In terms of coding, the ACA sped up the transition from:
a) CPT to HCPCS
b) ICD-9 to ICD-10
c) Stark Law to HIPAA
d) NCCI to CPT

28. Which of these is NOT a goal of the Affordable Care Act (ACA)?
a) Increase the quality and efficiency of healthcare
b) Promote fee-for-service healthcare models
c) Reduce health care costs
d) Ensure more Americans have access to quality health insurance

29. What is the primary goal of the Anti-Kickback Statute?
a) Prohibit payments for referrals
b) Protect patient information
c) Ensure proper coding procedures
d) Ensure all Americans have health insurance

30. The Security Rule of HIPAA is mainly focused on the protection of what type of information?
a) Personal contact details
b) Physician notes
c) Electronic Protected Health Information (ePHI)
d) Insurance claim details

31. Which organization accredits hospitals and ensures they meet specific criteria and standards for patient care and safety?
a) World Health Organization (WHO)
b) American Medical Association (AMA)
c) Centers for Disease Control and Prevention (CDC)
d) The Joint Commission

32. Which of the following best describes telemedicine?
a) Using technology for remote patient monitoring
b) Offering medical advice through phone calls
c) Delivering health services and information via digital communication tools
d) Using robots in surgical procedures

33. What is the primary goal of the Patient-Centered Medical Home (PCMH) model?
a) To reduce the cost of healthcare for patients
b) To focus on disease-specific treatments only
c) To coordinate care around the patient and improve health outcomes
d) To increase the number of primary care providers

34. Which of the following is NOT a core objective of Meaningful Use?
a) Enhancing quality, safety, and efficiency
b) Engaging patients and families in their health
c) Improving public health and population health management
d) Expanding the roles of nurses in patient care

35. In healthcare, what does HIE stand for?
a) Health Insurance Exchange
b) Health Information Economy
c) Health Insurance Exception
d) Health Information Exchange

36. Which federal Act was passed in 2009 to promote the adoption and meaningful use of health information technology?
a) Affordable Care Act (ACA)
b) Health Information Technology for Economic and Clinical Health (HITECH) Act
c) Patient Safety and Quality Improvement Act
d) Medicare Access and CHIP Reauthorization Act (MACRA)

37. A healthcare model that focuses on the simultaneous prevention and management of multiple chronic conditions is called:
a) Multimodal Care
b) Multipurpose Care
c) Multimorbidity Care
d) Multidisciplinary Care

38. The primary purpose of the National Practitioner Data Bank (NPDB) is to:
a) Store patient medical records
b) Provide a directory of all practicing physicians in the US
c) Enhance the quality of healthcare by reporting on medical malpractice payments and specific adverse actions
d) Offer a platform for doctors to collaborate on research

39. Which of the following focuses on ensuring that medical devices and software can exchange and interpret data?
a) Health Analytics
b) Device Interoperability
c) Digital Health Integration
d) Medical Device Usability

40. Which health policy introduced the "Donut Hole" concept in prescription drug coverage?
a) Affordable Care Act (ACA)
b) Medicare Part D
c) Health Savings Account (HSA)
d) Patient Protection Act

Answers Effective Medical Coding Techniques and Strategies

1. Answer: a. Current Procedural Terminology
Reason: The Current Procedural Terminology (CPT) is one of the primary coding systems used in the medical industry. Medical coders need to be familiar with the CPT, as well as other systems like the HCPCS and ICD, to ensure accurate code assignment and compliant medical billing.

2. Answer: b. Frequently complete coding tasks and case studies
Reason: Regularly engaging in coding tasks and case studies allows medical coders to apply their understanding of coding systems and guidelines practically. This hands-on experience ensures that coders remain proficient, understand the intricacies of the systems, and can make accurate assignments in real-world scenarios.

3. Answer: c. Open communication with healthcare professionals
Reason: Open and effective communication with healthcare providers is paramount in the coding process. This ensures that any discrepancies, unclear information, or additional documentation needed can be addressed promptly. Ensuring accurate coding is crucial for appropriate billing and patient care.

4. Answer: b. Using coding software and tools
Reason: Leveraging specialized software and tools designed for medical coding can enhance efficiency and accuracy. These tools often have built-in features to help streamline the coding process, offer suggestions, and validate assigned codes against coding standards.

5. Answer: c. Pursuing additional credentials and certifications
Reason: Acquiring additional credentials and certifications in the field of medical coding demonstrates an advanced level of expertise. This not only enhances the coder's skill set but also can open up new career opportunities and position them as experts in specific areas of medical coding.

6. Answer: c. Analyzing patient medical records in-depth
Reason: Thorough review and analysis of patient medical records are foundational to effective medical coding. This ensures that every relevant piece of information, such as symptoms, diagnoses, treatments, and other related data, is captured and coded correctly.

7. Answer: c. Professional organizations like AAPC and AHIMA
Reason: Associations like AAPC and AHIMA are dedicated to medical coding and provide a wealth of resources, educational opportunities, and networking events. Being part of these organizations ensures that coders are always abreast of the latest trends, standards, and best practices in the industry.

8. Answer: a. Regular Participation in fitness exercises
Reason: While maintaining good health is essential, fitness exercises are separate from ensuring coding accuracy and compliance. It's internal and external audits, continuous quality improvement efforts, and corrective action plans that are key to achieving and maintaining high standards in medical coding.

9. Answer: b. Clear and concise communication
Reason: When addressing discrepancies or seeking additional information, it's essential to be clear and concise to avoid any misunderstandings. This ensures that any clarifications provided by healthcare providers are based on accurate information, which in turn guarantees correct coding.

10. Answer: c. Becoming proficient in using EHR systems
Reason: Electronic Health Record (EHR) systems are integral in the modern healthcare industry. They contain a comprehensive record of patient data. Being proficient in using these systems allows coders to access, review, and code the required information efficiently.

11. Answer: b. Familiarity with coding systems and guidelines
Reason: The foundation of effective medical coding lies in an in-depth understanding of coding systems and guidelines. Familiarity with these ensures that coders can correctly translate patient data into appropriate codes, ensuring accurate billing and adherence to industry standards.

12. Answer: c. Online forums and social media groups dedicated to Medical Coding
Reason: Online communities provide a space for professionals to share experiences, insights, and advice. For medical coders, these platforms offer a valuable opportunity to learn from peers, ask questions, and stay updated on industry changes.

13. Answer: b. AI-driven game applications
Reason: While AI is becoming increasingly prominent in many industries, AI-driven game applications aren't tools used in medical coding. Instead, EHRs, coding software, and other specialized tools are essential for coders.

14. Answer: c. Coding performance metrics
Reason: Monitoring coding performance metrics, such as accuracy rates and claim denial rates, provides insights into the effectiveness of coding practices. Regularly tracking these metrics allows for timely identification and rectification of issues, ensuring high standards of coding.

15. Answer: c. Correctly evaluating patient record data
Reason: A deep understanding of medical jargon and acronyms is essential for accurately interpreting and coding patient data. This ensures that the coder captures the nuances of the medical data and translates it correctly into the relevant codes.

16. Answer: b. Establishing a systematic procedure for evaluating medical records
Reason: A systematic approach ensures that all pertinent patient data is captured during the coding process. It provides a structured method for reviewing records, ensuring that no relevant information is overlooked, which is critical for accurate coding.

17. Answer: d. International Medical Coders Association (IMCA)
Reason: The International Medical Coders Association (IMCA) is not commonly recognized as a major organization for professional networking among medical coders. The American Medical Association (AMA), American Academy of Professional Coders (AAPC), and American Health Information Management Association (AHIMA) are well-established and widely recognized organizations that provide resources, certification programs, and networking opportunities for medical coding professionals.

18. Answer: b. Relying solely on personal experience
Reason: Relying solely on personal experience is not an effective way to understand coding systems better. Coding systems are complex and constantly evolving, requiring coders to engage in ongoing education, use coding guides and online resources, and complete coding tasks and case studies frequently. Personal experience can complement these methods but should not be the sole basis for understanding and keeping up with coding standards.

19. Answer: c. coding software and tools
Reason: Coding software and tools offer automated code suggestions to assist in the coding process, making them invaluable for medical coders. These tools are designed to improve accuracy, efficiency, and compliance with coding standards. Unlike basic calculators, food recipe apps, or music streaming platforms, coding software and tools are specifically tailored to address the needs and challenges of medical coding.

20. Answer: b. Carefully reviewing every aspect of the medical record
Reason: To ensure that all pertinent data is captured during coding, medical coders must carefully review every aspect of the medical record. This includes doctor's notes, test results, and any other relevant documentation. Ignoring any part of the medical record or relying solely on specific types of data can lead to inaccuracies in coding, which can impact patient care and billing.

21. Answer: c. Discuss options for improving documentation with healthcare professionals
Reason: To promote more accurate coding, medical coders should engage in open communication with healthcare professionals to discuss options for improving documentation. This collaborative approach helps identify and address documentation gaps or ambiguities, leading to more accurate and comprehensive medical records, which are essential for effective coding.

22. Answer: a. Effective medical coding techniques
Reason: Effective medical coding techniques involve a combination of in-depth knowledge of coding systems, thorough analysis of medical records, and the use of technology to enhance accuracy and efficiency. This multidimensional strategy is critical for achieving high standards in medical coding, unlike basic first aid skills, advanced driving techniques, or gardening techniques, which are unrelated to the medical coding profession.

23. Answer: c. Attend industry conferences and events
Reason: To stay current with the latest medical coding trends, medical coders should attend industry conferences and events. These gatherings offer opportunities for learning, networking, and exposure to the latest developments and best practices in medical coding. Unlike avoiding industry events, attending comedy shows, or taking a break from the profession, participating in professional gatherings is a proactive way to maintain and enhance coding expertise.

24. Answer: c. Communicate with healthcare professionals for clarification
Reason: When faced with unclear information in patient records, medical coders should communicate with healthcare professionals for clarification. This ensures that coding is based on accurate and complete information, thereby reducing the risk of errors. Guessing the meaning, overlooking the data, or seeking input from unqualified sources can lead to inaccuracies and potentially compromise patient care and billing.

25. Answer: c. Advancements in AI and machine learning technologies
Reason: Advancements in AI and machine learning technologies have the potential to revolutionize the medical coding process by increasing accuracy, efficiency, and compliance. These technologies can automate routine tasks, provide code suggestions based on vast datasets, and identify patterns that may not be immediately apparent to human coders. Unlike novels, dreams, or crystal balls, AI and machine learning offer tangible benefits based on data analysis and computational power.

26. Answer: b. Completing coding tasks and case studies
Reason: Completing coding tasks and case studies helps medical coders put their understanding of coding systems into practice. This hands-on approach allows coders to apply theoretical knowledge in practical scenarios, honing their skills and improving their proficiency in real-world coding challenges. Unlike activities such as swimming, painting, or hiking, coding tasks and case studies are directly relevant to the development of coding expertise.

27. Answer: b. To ensure adherence to coding guidelines
Reason: Regular coding audits are conducted to ensure adherence to coding guidelines and identify areas for improvement. By systematically reviewing coding practices and records, audits help maintain high standards of accuracy and compliance, thereby enhancing the quality of patient care and financial integrity. Audits are not meant to create additional work without purpose, entertain staff, or serve merely as formalities.

28. Answer: c. Ignoring feedback and suggestions
Reason: Ignoring feedback and suggestions is not a way to improve documentation quality. On the contrary, clear communication with healthcare professionals, regular training on documentation best practices, and implementing corrective action plans are essential strategies for enhancing documentation. Feedback and suggestions provide valuable insights for identifying areas of improvement and fostering a culture of continuous learning and development.

29. Answer: b. Professional organizations like AAPC and AHIMA

Reason: Professional organizations like the American Academy of Professional Coders (AAPC) and the American Health Information Management Association (AHIMA) are key resources for medical coders seeking to understand evolving coding standards better. These organizations offer educational programs, certification courses, and updated guidelines that reflect the latest developments in medical coding. Unlike mystery novels, children's storybooks, or cookbooks, these professional organizations provide specific, relevant, and authoritative information for coding professionals.

30. Answer: b. Accurate code assignment

Reason: A primary goal for medical coders is to ensure accurate code assignment, which is crucial for accurate billing and insurance claims. Precise coding affects reimbursement rates, compliance with regulations, and the overall financial health of healthcare providers. Unlike efficient party planning, doodling in free time, or changing coding rules daily, accurate code assignment directly impacts the quality and integrity of the coding and billing process.

Answers Laws and Regulations

1. Answer: c) 1996

Reason: The Health Insurance Portability and Accountability Act (HIPAA) was established in 1996. It was designed to protect patient health information and ensure the portability of health insurance across job changes.

2. Answer: b) Electronic PHI

Reason: The Security Rule under HIPAA primarily concerns the protection of Electronic Protected Health Information (ePHI). This rule establishes national standards to safeguard the confidentiality, integrity, and availability of ePHI.

3. Answer: d) ABCD

Reason: The ABCD code set is not mandated by HIPAA. HIPAA does require the use of standardized code sets, such as ICD, CPT, and HCPCS, in electronic healthcare transactions.

4. Answer: c) Fraudulent government claims

Reason: The False Claims Act is aimed at targeting those who defraud governmental programs. It's designed to prevent and punish fraudulent claims made to the government, especially within the healthcare domain.

5. Answer: b) Payments for eligible patient referrals

Reason: The Anti-Kickback Statute was established to prevent financial incentives (kickbacks) in exchange for patient referrals or the recommendation of healthcare goods or services reimbursed by federal healthcare programs.

6. Answer: c) Doctors referring Medicare and Medicaid patients to entities they have business relationships with

Reason: Stark Law, or the Physician Self-Referral Law, prohibits physicians from referring patients to receive designated health services paid for by Medicare or Medicaid from entities with which the physician or an immediate family member has a financial relationship unless an exception applies.

7. Answer: c) CMS and NCHS

Reason: While the World Health Organization (WHO) publishes the ICD system for global use, in the US, the Centers for Medicare & Medicaid Services (CMS) and the National Center for Health Statistics (NCHS) modify it to fit the American health care context better.

8. Answer: d) AMA

Reason: The Current Procedural Terminology (CPT) Coding system was created by the American Medical Association (AMA). It's a set of codes used to describe medical, surgical, and diagnostic services provided by healthcare professionals.

9. Answer: c) Affordable Care Act (ACA)

Reason: The Affordable Care Act (ACA), passed in 2010, is commonly referred to as Obamacare. It was a significant overhaul of the US healthcare system, aimed at increasing the number of insured Americans, improving the quality and efficiency of healthcare, and reducing healthcare costs.

10. Answer: a) Protecting PHI

Reason: While the protection of PHI is essential in the healthcare domain and governed by acts like HIPAA, the primary objectives of the ACA are to expand access to health insurance, improve patient protections, emphasize health and wellness, improve quality, and reduce healthcare costs.

11. Answer: b) Value-based care

Reason: The Affordable Care Act (ACA) introduced measures to shift the US health care system from a fee-for-service model to a value-based care model. This model emphasizes the quality of care provided over the quantity of services rendered.

12. Answer: b) ICD-9 to ICD-10

Reason: The ACA played a role in accelerating the transition from the ICD-9 coding system to the more detailed and granular ICD-10 system, allowing for better tracking and categorization of diseases and treatments.

13. Answer: a) Disclosure of PHI

Reason: The HIPAA Privacy Rule dictates that the unauthorized disclosure of Protected Health Information (PHI) typically requires patient consent. While specific uses and disclosures of PHI for treatment, payment, and healthcare operations are allowed, others require explicit patient authorization.

14. Answer: c) Electronic Health Records (EHRs)

Reason: The ACA emphasized the importance of Electronic Health Records (EHRs) as a means to improve the quality of care, enhance patient safety, and reduce healthcare costs. EHRs enable seamless communication and information exchange between healthcare providers.

15. Answer: c) CMS

Reason: The Centers for Medicare & Medicaid Services (CMS) is the federal agency responsible for overseeing the Medicare and Medicaid programs in the US. It plays a crucial role in ensuring these programs serve their beneficiaries effectively.

16. Answer: c) Affordable Care Act (ACA)

Reason: The Affordable Care Act (ACA) introduced robust measures to prevent fraud, waste, and abuse in the healthcare system. Through various provisions, the ACA strengthened the federal government's capacity to fight fraud and impose stricter penalties for fraudulent activities.

17. Answer: b) Developing a skilled healthcare workforce

Reason: The ACA provided funding for projects that aim to develop a highly skilled healthcare workforce. A well-trained workforce is essential for the delivery of high-quality health care and to meet the challenges of a rapidly changing healthcare environment.

18. Answer: d) HIPAA Privacy Rule

Reason: The HIPAA Privacy Rule is the benchmark for the protection of patient medical records and other Protected Health Information (PHI). It establishes the conditions under which PHI can be used and disclosed and ensures patients' rights over their information.

19. Answer: c) Fee-for-service to value-based

Reason: One of the primary changes driven by the ACA was the shift in focus from the traditional fee-for-service care models, where providers are paid for each service rendered, to value-based care models, where payment is based on the overall quality and outcome of the care provided.

20. Answer: b) Ensure proper use of coding procedures

Reason: The National Correct Coding Initiative (NCCI) was implemented to promote correct coding methodologies and to control improper coding leading to inappropriate payment. Its goal is to ensure that medical coding is done accurately and consistently.

21. Answer: c) CMS

Reason: The Centers for Medicare & Medicaid Services (CMS) is housed within the US Department of Health and Human Services (HHS). It's responsible for the administration of significant healthcare programs like Medicare, Medicaid, and the Children's Health Insurance Program (CHIP).

22. Answer: b) ICD-10

Reason: ICD-10 provides a higher level of detail and granularity than its predecessor, ICD-9. This increased level of detail allows for more accurate patient care tracking, better data for epidemiological studies, and improved billing accuracy.

23. Answer: b) Physician self-referrals

Reason: The Stark Law specifically addresses physician self-referrals. It prohibits physicians from referring patients to receive designated health services paid for by Medicare or Medicaid from entities with which the physician or a close family member has a financial relationship unless an exception applies.

24. Answer: c) AMA

Reason: The Current Procedural Terminology (CPT) Coding system was created by the American Medical Association (AMA). It serves as a uniform language for describing the medical, surgical, and diagnostic services provided by healthcare professionals and is widely used for billing purposes.

25. Answer: b) Value-based care

Reason: The Affordable Care Act (ACA) promotes a shift towards value-based care. Unlike fee-for-service models, which focus on the quantity of services provided, value-based care emphasizes the quality of care, aiming for better patient outcomes, and reduced healthcare costs.

26. Answer: c) Entities physicians have financial relationships with

Reason: The Stark Law specifically focuses on entities with which physicians have financial relationships. It prohibits these physicians from referring Medicare and Medicaid patients to such entities for designated health services unless an exception applies.

27. Answer: b) ICD-9 to ICD-10

Reason: One of the changes brought about by the ACA was the transition from ICD-9 to ICD-10 coding systems. This was done to enhance the specificity of clinical data captured, allowing for better patient care management and more accurate billing practices.

28. Answer: b) Promote fee-for-service healthcare models

Reason: The ACA does not aim to promote fee-for-service healthcare models. Instead, one of its main objectives is to shift the healthcare system towards a value-based care model, where quality of care and patient outcomes are prioritized over the volume of services rendered.

29. Answer: a) Prohibit payments for referrals

Reason: The Anti-Kickback Statute's primary objective is to prohibit payments made in exchange for patient referrals or for the recommendation of healthcare goods or services reimbursed by federal healthcare programs. The statute is in place to ensure that decisions about patient care are based on the best interests of the patient rather than financial incentives.

30. Answer: c) Electronic Protected Health Information (ePHI)

Reason: The Security Rule of HIPAA is primarily concerned with the protection of Electronic Protected Health Information (ePHI). It sets standards for ensuring the confidentiality, integrity, and availability of ePHI, protecting patient data in an increasingly digital healthcare environment.

31. Answer: d. The Joint Commission

Reason: The Joint Commission is an independent, non-profit organization that accredits and certifies more than 21,000 healthcare organizations and programs in the United States. It focuses on ensuring that these institutions meet specific standards for patient care and safety. While organizations like the WHO, AMA, and CDC have their essential roles in healthcare, accrediting hospitals is a primary function of The Joint Commission.

32. Answer: c. Delivering health services and information via digital communication tools

Reason: Telemedicine encompasses a broad range of services, not just remote patient monitoring or offering advice over the phone. It involves the use of digital communication tools, including video conferencing, to diagnose, consult, treat, and educate patients remotely. While technology might play a role in surgeries (option d), that is more about telehealth and robotic surgery than the broader concept of telemedicine.

33. Answer: c. To coordinate care around the patient and improve health outcomes

Reason: The Patient-Centered Medical Home (PCMH) model emphasizes care coordination and communication to transform primary care into "what patients want it to be." It revolves around the patient and aims to improve health outcomes by using evidence-based medicine and clinical decision-support tools. While cost-effectiveness and provider numbers are essential in healthcare, they aren't the primary goals of the PCMH model.

34. Answer: d. Expanding the roles of nurses in patient care

Reason: The core objectives of Meaningful Use pertain to promoting the widespread adoption of Electronic Health Records (EHRs) and leveraging them to improve patient care outcomes. The main objectives are improving quality, safety, and efficiency, reducing health disparities, engaging patients and families, improving care coordination, and ensuring adequate privacy and security of patient health information. The expansion of nursing roles is essential in healthcare but isn't a core objective of Meaningful Use.

35. Answer: d. Health Information Exchange

Reason: Health Information Exchange (HIE) pertains to the electronic movement of health-related data among organizations according to nationally recognized standards. It aims to facilitate access to and retrieval of clinical data to provide safer, timelier, efficient, effective, equitable, patient-centered care.

36. Answer: b. Health Information Technology for Economic and Clinical Health (HITECH) Act

Reason: The HITECH Act was enacted in 2009 as part of the American Recovery and Reinvestment Act. It promotes the adoption and meaningful use of health information technology, especially electronic health records. While other acts like the ACA have provisions related to health IT, the HITECH Act was explicitly centered on this subject.

37. Answer: c. Multimorbidity Care

Reason: Multimorbidity refers to the presence of two or more chronic conditions in an individual. In a healthcare context, Multimorbidity Care aims at an integrated approach to simultaneously prevent and manage multiple chronic conditions, considering the complexity of patients' needs rather than treating each disease in isolation.

38. Answer: c. Enhance the quality of healthcare by reporting on medical malpractice payments and specific adverse actions

Reason: The National Practitioner Data Bank (NPDB) is a repository of reports containing information on medical malpractice payments and specific adverse actions related to healthcare practitioners, providers, and suppliers. It serves as a reference for entities like hospitals and licensing boards to promote quality healthcare and protect the public.

39. Answer: b. Device Interoperability

Reason: Device Interoperability in healthcare refers to the capability of different information technology systems and medical devices to connect, exchange data, and collaborate in a coordinated manner, internally and externally. This ensures that medical devices and software can effectively share and interpret data, optimizing patient care.

40. Answer: b. Medicare Part D

Reason: Medicare Part D, which provides prescription drug coverage, introduced the "Donut Hole" or coverage gap. This refers to a temporary limit on what the drug plan will cover for drugs. After a beneficiary and their plan have spent a certain amount on covered drugs, they enter this coverage gap, during which they pay more out-of-pocket for prescriptions until they reach the catastrophic coverage phase.

Q & A WITH EXPLANATIONS

Medical coding is crucial in the constantly changing healthcare industry. That guarantees correct billing and effective communication between healthcare professionals. The section "Questions and Answers - Understanding the Intricacies of Medical Coding" thoroughly examines the most typical queries and in-depth responses about medical coding. Readers will better grasp the coding procedure, industry standards, and the function of medical coders in the healthcare system by the end of this chapter.

Questions on Use of billing codes

What possible repercussions could arise from using inaccurate or out-of-date billing codes in medical coding?
Utilizing inaccurate or out-of-date billing codes may lead to the denial of claims, under- or overpayment of fees, problems with compliance, and legal ramifications.

How do medical coders choose the appropriate billing codes for a specific medical service?
Medical coders must examine the medical documentation to assign the proper billing codes and find the pertinent diagnoses, procedures, and services.

What are the advantages and disadvantages of adopting CAC technology for medical coding?
Although CAC technology can increase coding productivity and accuracy, it also necessitates a sizable initial investment, continuing upkeep, and quality control procedures.

While employing billing codes, how do medical coders adhere to the Health Insurance Portability and Accountability Act (HIPAA)?
When assigning billing codes, medical coders must ensure that they are not divulging any protected health information (PHI) and are abiding by HIPAA rules for storing and sending PHI.

How do medical coders manage intricate medical cases with several diagnoses and treatments?
Before assigning codes for any additional diagnoses or pertinent procedures, medical coders must carefully review the medical paperwork to identify the main cause of the medical treatment.

What typical issues do medical coders encounter while coding for mental health services?
Due to the complexity of mental health diagnoses, the need to distinguish between acute and chronic disorders, and the demand for additional paperwork to prove medical necessity, coding for mental health services can be difficult.

Using hierarchical condition categories (HCCs) in medical coding has advantages and disadvantages, state that.
HCCs can assist in identifying and prioritizing patients with complicated medical diseases for further care management and reimbursement. Still, they also demand a lot of skill and resources to be implemented successfully.

What potential moral dilemmas could medical coders encounter while choosing billing codes?

Medical coders must ensure that the medical services they portray are accurate and not assign codes to patients' detriment to maximize reimbursement.

What are the best procedures for checking the compliance and correctness of medical coding?

Audits should be conducted regularly and methodically to discover patterns and trends using retrospective reviews, peer reviews, and data analysis.

What are the medical billing and coding industry's current trends and plans?

Artificial intelligence and electronic health records are currently on the rise. In the future, there may be more cooperation between payers and healthcare providers to improve reimbursement and lighten administrative responsibilities.

Questions on Effective Medical Coding techniques and strategies

What are the fundamental ideas behind efficient medical coding, and how may they assist in guaranteeing appropriate payment for healthcare services?

ICD-10, CPT, and HCPCS are some pertinent coding systems that must be understood to code medical records effectively. To succeed, coders must communicate effectively with physicians and other healthcare professionals, stay up to date on changes to coding standards and procedures, and pay special attention to detail when analyzing patient and medical data.

How can coders guarantee that medical records are efficiently and accurately coded?

Coders should concentrate on correctness and completeness, employing coding software and other tools to help speed up the process of coding medical records correctly and efficiently. Also, they should be conversant with the coding standards for each system they use and constantly evaluate their work to find and fix problems.

What typical coding mistakes can result in incorrect reimbursement or claims being rejected?

The use of inappropriate codes, improper service documentation, and the absence of or inadequate documentation are examples of common coding errors. These mistakes may expose healthcare providers to legal and regulatory problems and lead to refused claims or delayed reimbursements.

What methods may healthcare providers employ to ensure their coding procedures adhere to legal and regulatory standards?

Healthcare professionals can use many tactics to ensure their coding procedures adhere to legal and regulatory requirements. These can involve creating and implementing coding policies and processes, supplying coding workers with ongoing training, and routinely evaluating coding practices to find and fix problems.

How can healthcare providers improve their coding procedures to increase reimbursement and reduce the possibility of having claims rejected?

Healthcare providers should concentrate on accuracy and completeness while optimizing their coding procedures, ensuring that all pertinent services are accurately documented and coded. They should also work closely with coders to ensure they have the tools and assistance they need to accomplish their jobs well and keep up with changes to coding regulations and guidelines.

What are some recommended practices for coding complex medical situations like chronic conditions?

It might be difficult to code chronic diseases and other complicated medical situations, but several best practices can assist in guaranteeing correctness and thoroughness. Ensure that all services are accurately documented and classified; this may entail evaluating all pertinent medical records and documentation, collaborating closely with doctors and other healthcare professionals, and remaining current on coding legislation and norms changes.

What steps should programmers take to ensure their work complies with HIPAA rules and other privacy laws?

When handling medical records and patient information, coders should follow stringent privacy and security measures to ensure their work complies with HIPAA rules and other privacy laws. Using secure coding software and other tools, adhering to stringent access control measures, and routinely evaluating and upgrading their policies and processes to ensure compliance with the most recent requirements are a few examples of what this might include.

What are some recommended procedures for telemedicine and other virtual medical visits?

It might be difficult to accurately and completely code telemedicine services and other virtual medical consultations, but a few recommended practices can help. These can involve keeping up with changes to coding standards and laws about telemedicine, recording all pertinent services and processes, and utilizing the proper codes for virtual medical visits.

How can healthcare professionals use coding data to raise the standard of care and patient outcomes?

To make data-driven patient care and treatment decisions, healthcare providers can use coding data to spot trends and patterns in patient outcomes and care quality. This can entail following patient outcomes over time, reviewing coding data to find areas for improvement, and using coding data to guide clinical judgment.

What new medical coding trends exist, and how can healthcare professionals prepare for them?

The adoption of value-based payment models, which put the quality of care above the number of services, the increased use of artificial intelligence and machine learning to streamline coding procedures, and the expanding significance of interoperability and data exchange in healthcare are all emerging trends in medical coding.

Healthcare providers should invest in technology and training to ensure that their coding procedures are current and in compliance with the most recent rules and guidelines to be prepared for these changes. They should also collaborate closely with coders and other medical specialists to pinpoint problem areas and implement plans to enhance coding procedures and patient outcomes. To stay on top of the curve, healthcare professionals also need to keep up with new developments in medical coding and healthcare legislation and modify their procedures accordingly.

Questions on Examples of Medical Coding cases

How should the codes be applied when a patient has diabetes and hypertension?
The ailment being treated as the main cause for the visit should be noted first when classifying coexisting conditions. For instance, list the diabetes code (E08-E13) first, then the hypertension code if that is the patient's main worry (I10-I16).

Since the healing process is unknown, how should fractures be coded?
Use the seventh character, "D," for subsequent treatment when coding fractures without information on the healing process to denote that the fracture is in an undetermined stage of healing.

What codes should a coder use for a patient with emphysema and chronic bronchitis?
J44.0 (a chronic obstructive pulmonary disease with an acute lower respiratory infection) or J44.9 (chronic obstructive pulmonary disease, unspecified) would be the correct codes for a patient who has both chronic bronchitis (J41-J42) and emphysema (J43).

Which guidelines are relevant for patients with diabetes who have both Type 1 and Type 2?
Diabetes Types 1 and 2 cannot coexist in the same individual. When the diagnosis is unclear, utilize code E13 (other specified diabetes mellitus) until the correct diagnosis is made.

How should chronic acute systolic heart failure be coded?
I50.23 is the code for acute-on-chronic systolic heart failure (acute on chronic systolic (congestive) heart failure), which includes both the acute and chronic aspects of the illness.

What code goes on an excisional biopsy for a breast lesion?
To represent an excisional biopsy of a breast lesion, use code 19125 (Excision of breast lesion diagnosed by the preoperative placement of radiological marker, open; single lesion).

How should a case be coded when a patient has both generalized anxiety disorder and major depressive illness?
Generalized anxiety disorder (F41.1) and major depressive disorder (F32.0-F33.9) need to be recorded separately. Prioritizing the primary reason for the visit over the other codes is advised.

What codes apply to a laparoscopic cholecystectomy?
Laparoscopic cholecystectomy is a minimally invasive surgical procedure that removes the gallbladder; it should be classified as 47562 (Laparoscopy, surgical; cholecystectomy).

How is a layered closure for repairing a laceration coded?
The nature and location of the wound closure determines the laceration repair codes. For a multilayer closure, use the codes 12001–13160, keeping in mind the accurate anatomical location and length of the laceration.

Which codes should the coder use for pressure ulcers and cellulitis patients?
Code the cellulitis (L89) under the designated site and stage, and code the pressure ulcer separately (L03) with the relevant anatomical site and location. Prioritizing the primary reason for the visit over the other codes is advised.

Questions on Industry legislation

What is the primary objective of the legislation that controls the medical coding sector?

The main objectives of industry guidelines for medical coding are establishing standard operating processes, protecting patient information, ensuring accurate medical billing, and maintaining legal compliance to prevent misuse and fraud.

Which American statute mandates the use of ICD-10-CM and ICD-10-PCS codes by medical coders?

In the United States, the Health Insurance Portability and Accountability Act (HIPAA) of 1996 mandates using ICD-10-CM for diagnoses and ICD-10-PCS for inpatient treatments.

What role does the False Claims Act have for medical coding?

When medical professionals make false or fraudulent claims about government healthcare programs—which can happen due to improper medical billing or coding practices—they are held accountable under the False Claims Act.

Which organization is in charge of updating and maintaining CPT codes?

The Current Procedural Terminology (CPT) codes used to describe medical operations and services are maintained and updated by the American Medical Association (AMA).

ICD, CPT, and HCPCS codes are updated how frequently?

ICD codes are changed once a year, while CPT and HCPCS Level II codes are updated yearly, with sporadic adjustments made as needed throughout the year.

National Correct Coding Initiative (NCCI) was founded in accordance with which U.S. statute?

The Omnibus Budget Reconciliation Act (OBRA) of 1990 created the National Correct Coding Initiative to encourage accurate coding and prevent fraudulent billing.

Compliance with medical coding is the responsibility of the Office of Inspector General (OIG).

A key responsibility of the OIG is to spot and deal with waste, fraud, and abuse in federal healthcare programs. The medical billing and coding procedures must adhere to rules and regulations.

HEAT's mission is to prevent and prosecute health care fraud. What does the team aim to achieve?

On HEAT, the United States and Canada have collaborated. Departments of Justice and Health and Human Services are tackling healthcare fraud, including incorrect medical coding and billing procedures.

As a result of the Affordable Care Act, how does medical coding change?

Medical coding procedures that are accurate and legal are enhanced by the Affordable Care Act and the implementation of electronic health records.

How does the American Health Information Management Association (AHIMA) influence medical coding?

Professional association called AHIMA helps the medical coding sector by giving health information management specialists tools, education, certification, and advocacy.

What role does the HIPAA Privacy Regulation play for medical coders?

A tight set of requirements must be followed by medical coders to maintain the security and confidentiality of patient data, according to the HIPAA Privacy Rule, which specifies standards for the protection of patients' personal health information.

What sanctions apply if medical coding regulations are broken?

Failure to abide by rules governing medical coding may incur financial fines, loss of billing rights, exclusion from government healthcare programs, and in certain circumstances, criminal prosecution.

Questions on Federal and state regulations

What do federal guidelines for medical coding serve?

To improve patient care, billing accuracy, and data collecting for research and quality assurance, federal standards for medical coding serve to standardize the classification and documentation of medical services and procedures.

What part do the Centers for Medicare and Medicaid Services (CMS) play in regulating medical coding?

The CMS is in charge of defining and maintaining code sets, putting payment mechanisms in place, running audits, and overseeing the enforcement of federal laws governing medical coding.

How do healthcare providers get affected by federal restrictions on medical coding?

When filing claims to Medicare, Medicaid, and private insurance companies, healthcare practitioners must adhere to federal requirements for medical coding by using the proper codes and documentation standards.

What are a few typical medical coding infractions?

Upcoding (billing for a higher level of service than was provided), unbundling (charging for different treatments that should be billed together), and inadequate documentation are common medical coding infractions.

What part do state laws play in medical coding?

Federal laws for medical coding may be supplemented by state regulations that impose additional reporting or documentation requirements or fines for noncompliance.

What distinguishes ICD-10-CM from ICD-10-PCS codes?

ICD-10-PCS codes are used to categorize processes and services, whereas ICD-10-CM codes are used to categorize diagnoses and symptoms.

What function does the NCCI (National Correct Coding Initiative) serve?

By identifying and preventing erroneous code combinations, the NCCI is a program created by CMS to improve nationwide consistency in coding and billing processes.

What are some essential medical coding documentation requirements?
The documentation must demonstrate the medical necessity of the services rendered and be accurate, thorough, and clear. The providers must also document any problems or comorbidities that may impact the patient's care.

What distinguishes a claim edit from a claim denial?
A denial is rejecting a claim due to errors or noncompliance with coding and billing laws. In contrast, a claim edit is a warning that a claim may have errors or inconsistencies that could result in a denial.

How can healthcare professionals ensure that medical coding is done under federal and state regulations?
Healthcare providers can maintain compliance by keeping up with coding and documentation standards, training employees, conducting routine audits, and executing corrective action plans as necessary.

Questions on Compliance processes

What are the main advantages of electronic health record (EHR) systems for medical coding?
EHR systems improve data accessibility, accuracy, and efficiency while lowering the chance of human mistakes and eliminating manual labor, which results in more accurate and efficient medical coding procedures.

How does Natural Language Processing (NLP) advance the field of medical coding?
To assign codes automatically, NLP algorithms evaluate and interpret the human language in clinical papers. This increases speed and accuracy while lightening the workload of medical coders.

What function does Computer-Assisted Coding (CAC) serve in medical coding?
CAC software dramatically reduces manual coding labor and boosts efficiency by analyzing clinical paperwork, finding pertinent codes, and suggesting precise ICD, CPT, and HCPCS codes.

How does using mobile applications help with medical coding?
Mobile apps for medical coding enable faster, more precise code lookups and increase overall coding efficiency by giving users access to code databases while on the road.

What function do tools for code validation in medical coding technology serve?
Code validation systems cross-check issued codes against official coding guidelines to confirm their accuracy and conformity, helping to avoid claim denials brought on by coding errors.

How much does machine learning (ML) enhance the medical coding process?
Correct code can be predicted and suggested by ML algorithms, making the coding process more efficient and lowering the risk of coding errors.

What role do application programming interfaces (APIs) play in medical coding technology?
APIs enable smooth data exchange between multiple healthcare systems, enabling access to vital data for medical coding tools and providing a more efficient and accurate coding procedure.

How do cloud-based technologies for medical coding improve the coding process?
Cloud-based technologies increase the overall efficiency and accuracy of the medical coding process by providing real-time access to updated code databases, facilitating coder cooperation, and providing safe storage and backups.

What function does encoder software serve in medical coding?
By providing thorough code search functionality, instructions, and decision-support features, encoder software aids coders in locating the most exact codes, increasing the accuracy of the coding process.

How does data analytics advance the field of medical coding?
Data analytics provides insights that enable continuous improvement of the medical coding process and lower the likelihood of errors and claim denials. It does this by identifying trends and patterns in coding practices.

What are the benefits of adopting specialist codebooks while coding for the medical field?
Comprehensive and current code listings are provided by specialized codebooks for various medical specialties, improving the efficiency and accuracy of code assignments in those professions.

How might artificial intelligence (AI) assist in adherence to medical codes?
AI can examine massive amounts of clinical documentation to find coding irregularities, fraud, and anomalies, improving coding compliance and lowering the likelihood of claim denials.

What role does routine software maintenance play in medical coding technology?
Frequent software upgrades make sure that coding tools are up to date with the most recent industry standards, legal requirements, and coding rules, ensuring the process' correctness and compliance.

How might collaborative tools enhance the process of medical coding?
Coders can collaborate, share expertise, and seek help from experts when using collaboration technologies, which encourages more accurate and efficient coding and lowers the risk of errors.

What function does ongoing education services in the field of medical coding technology?
medical coder can use the most recent tools and techniques to maintain a high degree of accuracy and speed in the medical coding process by staying current with the newest coding requirements, industry trends, and technological improvements through continuous education.

Questions on Tools and technology

What varieties of medical coding systems are employed in healthcare?
ICD-10-CM, CPT, and HCPCS are the three primary medical coding systems used in healthcare.

How is ICD-10-CM coding used in the healthcare industry? What is it?
The ICD-10-CM coding system categorizes and codes medical diagnoses and illnesses. For payment and data analysis, healthcare providers and insurance firms use it.

How is CPT coding utilized in the healthcare industry? What is it?
The CPT coding system categorizes and codes medical services and procedures. For payment and data analysis, healthcare providers and insurance firms use it.

How is HCPCS coding utilized in the healthcare industry?
The HCPCS coding system categorizes and codes medical supplies, equipment, and products. For payment and data analysis, healthcare providers and insurance firms use it.

What function does medical coding software serve in the medical field?
Healthcare professionals and coders employ medical coding software to accurately and efficiently code medical diagnoses, procedures, and products for payment and data analysis.

What advantages do electronic health records (EHRs) have for medical coding?
EHRs can facilitate quick and accurate access to patient data and medical histories for healthcare professionals and coders, increasing coding productivity and accuracy.

How does natural language processing (NLP) apply to medical coding?
NLP, a subfield of artificial intelligence, enables computers to comprehend and evaluate human language. It assists in automating the coding process and enhancing accuracy in medical coding.

Why is optical character recognition (OCR) employed in medical coding, and what is OCR?
OCR is a method for turning printed or handwritten text into digital text. It is employed in medical coding to facilitate the digitization of medical records and enhance coding precision.

How is computer-assisted coding (CAC) applied in medical coding?
The answer is that CAC is a system that suggests codes for medical diagnoses and procedures using algorithms and machine learning. It is utilized in medical coding to enhance speed and accuracy.

What impact will artificial intelligence (AI) have on medical coding?
The process of automating code can increase coding efficiency and correctness. For study and analysis, it can also assist in locating patterns and trends in medical data.

What are some of the difficulties in medical coding?
Coding errors, complexity, and modifications to coding rules and guidelines are some of the difficulties medical coders face.

How can medical service providers guarantee precise medical coding?
Healthcare professionals may ensure correct medical coding by using licensed and trained coders and complete documentation of patient diagnoses, treatments, and products.

What are some medical coding best practices?
The use of current coding standards, continual training and education for coders, regular audits of coding procedures, and accurate and detailed documentation are all examples of best practices for medical coding.

How do healthcare institutions make sure that coding rules and guidelines are followed?
Healthcare businesses ensure compliance with coding standards and guidelines by routinely assessing coding methods, offering continuous training and education for coders, and keeping up with coding updates and changes.

What part does medical coding play in the study of healthcare data?
Medical coding plays a significant role in the analysis of healthcare data by providing standardized codes for diagnoses, procedures, and goods that may be used to assess healthcare trends, outcomes, and expenditures.

Questions on Data management software

What does data management software entail when it comes to medical coding?
To ensure correct and consistent medical coding, data management software is a computer application that allows for collecting, storing, retrieving, and analyzing medical data.

Data management software is crucial for medical coding, so why?
Because precision and uniformity in medical coding are essential for invoicing, insurance claims, and patient care, data management software is significant for medicine.

Data management software's contribution to medical coding?
To make it simpler for medical coders to recognize and assign the proper codes to medical operations and diagnoses, data management software offers a systematic framework for collecting, storing, and retrieving medical data.

What advantages does adopting data management software for medical coding offer?
Using data management software for medical coding has several advantages, including increased consistency and accuracy in coding, faster coding procedures, fewer billing and insurance claim errors, and delays, and enhanced patient care through better data analysis.

Which well-known data management programs are utilized for medical coding?
The following are some well-known data management programs for medical coding: Epic, Cerner, Meditech, and Allscripts.

How do medical coders employ data management tools in their daily work?
Medical coders employ data management software to access patient data, assign medical codes to diagnoses and treatments, and guarantee coding accuracy and consistency.

What difficulties do medical coders have when utilizing data management software?
Medical coders might need help managing massive amounts of data, navigating intricate software interfaces, and maintaining data confidentiality and privacy.

What are some essential characteristics to search for in data management software for medical coding?
The capability to perform data analytics is one of the essential qualities to look for in data management software for medical coding, along with ease of use, accuracy, and consistency in coding.

How can data management software better the results for patients?
To evaluate patient data and spot patterns and trends in diagnosis and treatment outcomes, medical personnel can use data management software to enhance patient outcomes.

What effect has data management software made on the medical field?
The improvement of billing and insurance procedures, more precise and efficient medical coding, and improved patient outcomes have all been made possible by data management software.

What moral issues should be considered while using data management software for medical coding?
To ensure that medical judgments are founded on accurate and impartial data, data privacy and security, openness in data use, and other ethical issues must be considered while using data management software for medical coding.

What steps are involved in integrating data management software with other healthcare technologies?
To build a more cohesive and effective healthcare system, data management software can be connected with other medical technology, including electronic health records (EHRs), telemedicine platforms, and patient portals.

What function does artificial intelligence (AI) perform in medical coding data management software?
Integrating AI in data management software for medical coding can increase coding accuracy and consistency and automate tedious coding operations.

How can data management tools be applied to advance medical research?
By enabling researchers to access and evaluate substantial amounts of medical data and to spot patterns and trends in diagnoses and treatment outcomes, data management software can be utilized to enhance healthcare research.

What possible advancements in data management software for medical coding are there?
The use of blockchain technology for secure data sharing, the incorporation of machine learning and AI for improved coding accuracy and efficiency, and the development of more user-friendly interfaces for more straightforward navigation and data analysis are potential future developments in data management software for medical coding. Moreover, improvements in speech recognition and natural language processing (NLP) technologies may make data entering and coding more accessible and practical. Overall, the future of data management software for medical coding appears bright, thanks to ongoing technological improvements that make medical coding more accurate and efficient and eventually lead to better patient outcomes.

Questions on Automation Tools

How have automated tools increased the accuracy of medical coding?
Automation systems have boosted medical coding accuracy by removing human error and inconsistent coding, decreasing coding errors, and speeding the coding process.

Which automation tools are most frequently employed in medical coding?
Computer-assisted coding (CAC) software, natural language processing (NLP) tools, and machine learning techniques are frequently used automation technologies in medical coding.

How does software for computer-assisted coding function?
To assess clinical documentation and recommend suitable medical codes, CAC software combines rule-based algorithms with machine learning.

What benefits can NLP offer to medical coding?
NLP technologies examine unstructured data, such as free text, to find pertinent medical phrases and convert them into medical codes.

What advantages can medical coding automation software offer?
Automation systems can boost coding accuracy, and productivity, cut expenses, and guarantee regulatory compliance.

How do automation tools support medical billing processes?
By creating correct invoices and electronically sending claims to insurance providers, automation solutions help speed up the medical billing process.

What role might automation solutions play in managing the revenue cycle for healthcare providers?
By enhancing coding accuracy, lowering claim denials, and accelerating payment collections, automation systems can assist providers in managing their revenue cycle.

What are the essential characteristics of medical coding automation tools?
Integration with existing systems, ease of use, adaptability, and scalability are essential for automation solutions.

How might automation tools enhance patient care?
To reduce coding errors, automation tools are used in patient care. As a result, clinical documentation is enhanced, and healthcare professionals are better able to make decisions.

What are the potential drawbacks of using automated technologies for medical coding excessively?
Overreliance on technology, errors brought on by flawed algorithms, and limited career possibilities for medical coders are potential drawbacks of using automation tools excessively.

How can healthcare providers guarantee that automation tools are applied to medical coding responsibly?
Providers may make sure automation technologies are used responsibly by putting quality control systems in place, monitoring performance, and verifying and testing algorithms.

How do automation tools impact the work of medical coders?
Automation tools may change the nature of work for medical coders, but it is doubtful that human intervention in the coding process will become obsolete.

Is it possible to improve medical coding in behavioral health and psychiatry using automated techniques?

Automated methods can be applied to improve medical coding accuracy in behavioral health and psychiatry, among other professions.

How can medical practitioners stay on top of changing coding regulations using automation tools?

To stay updated with evolving coding rules, providers can use automation solutions by integrating systems that regularly get updates from code authorities.

What forms will medical coding automation tools take in the future?

Accuracy and productivity gains in medical coding automation systems are expected to be accompanied by an increase in AI and machine learning use.

Questions on Career advice

How can I determine if a job in medical coding is right for me?

If medical coding is a career that aligns with your beliefs, talents, and interests, it might be a good fit for you. Medical coding necessitates clear communication, critical thinking, and meticulous attention to detail. You'll need to keep up with changing regulations and understand medical terminology and coding procedures. Consider your talents, speak with experts, and conduct a study to determine if this career suits you.

What are the fundamental skills required to succeed in medical coding?

Medical coding requires high attention to detail, critical thinking, efficient communication, and familiarity with medical language and coding procedures. To accurately code medical diagnoses and techniques, you need to be detail-oriented and able to handle complex information. It also requires analytical thinking because you must examine medical records and come to judgments based on data. Working with insurance companies and healthcare providers calls for practical communication skills.

What type of education is required to become a medical coder?

To work as a medical coder, most companies require a high school diploma or its equivalent in addition to the successful completion of a certification program in medical coding. Anatomy, physiology, and medical terminology are some of the subjects taught in certification programs, which last six to twelve months on average. An associate's or bachelor's degree in health information management or a related field may also be necessary for specific jobs.

What advantages can medical coding certifications offer?

A medical coding certification can enhance employment opportunities, boost income potential, and show more significant subject matter experience. Your certification demonstrates that you have attained a specified proficiency level and are qualified for the position. Applying for jobs and negotiating salaries provides you with an advantage.

What employment options are there for medical coders?

Hospitals, clinics, insurance firms, and governmental organizations are just some places where medical coders can find employment. Some programmers may operate alone or remotely. Medical coder, a specialist in coding, supervisor, or manager are all possible job titles. Additionally, there are chances to progress, such as by working as a coding educator or taking a managerial role.

What is the future of the medical coding field?

The Bureau of Labor Statistics projects that the employment of medical record and health information technologists, including medical coders, will increase by 8% between 2019 and 2029, faster than the average for all occupations. Medical coders will be required more frequently to handle and organize health information as the population ages and healthcare demand rises.

What is the medical coding industry's average salary?
In May 2020, the median annual pay for medical records and health information technologists (which includes medical coders) was $44,090, according to the Bureau of Labor Statistics. Location, employer, amount of experience, and qualification are some variables that affect earnings.

What typical difficulties do medical coders encounter?
Working with missing or erroneous medical records, coping with a high amount of work, and meeting deadlines are all common issues medical coders face.

What are some pointers for keeping up with medical coding trends?
Consider joining professional organizations, attending conferences and workshops, reading trade magazines, and participating in online forums and discussion groups to stay up to date on medical coding. Moreover, networking with other industry experts and looking for further training and education possibilities might be beneficial.

What are some possible professions for medical coders?
Medical coders may work as coding managers or supervisors, educators or trainers, consultants or auditors, or healthcare data analysts. Some coders might also focus on a specific field, like oncology or cardiology coding.

How can I be ready for a medical coding job interview?
To prepare for a job interview in medical coding:

1. Learn about the business and become familiar with their coding practices and software platforms.
2. Examine your resume, and be ready to talk about your experience and credentials.
3. Be prepared to talk about your understanding of medical jargon and coding practices, attention to detail, and capacity for autonomy and teamwork.

Which software programs are frequently used in medical coding?
The software platforms Epic, Cerner, Meditech, and 3M are frequently used in medical coding. These programs provide medical record management, code assignment, and interaction with insurance and healthcare providers.

What are the recommended procedures for medical coders to guarantee efficiency and accuracy?
Medical coders should follow best practices such as double-checking codes for accuracy, remaining current on coding legislation and norms, being clear when dealing with healthcare providers and insurance companies, and using software and tools to speed up the coding process.

What ethical issues are there with medical coding?

Maintaining patient confidentiality, ensuring that codes accurately reflect the services rendered, and avoiding dishonest or abusive coding techniques are all ethical considerations in medical coding. Coders must also abide by the standards set forth by their professional associations and keep abreast of any amendments to the laws and regulations governing healthcare security and privacy.

What techniques may medical coders use to sharpen their coding abilities?

Medical coders might participate in continuing education courses, seek mentorship or coaching from more seasoned coders, take coding examinations and quizzes, and practice coding scenarios and case studies to hone their coding skills. Through professional associations and trade periodicals, it can also be helpful to keep up with coding standards and market trends.

Questions on Required skills and competencies

How significant is accuracy in medical coding?

Medical coding requires dealing with complex healthcare data and allocating codes to distinct diseases and treatments. Thus accuracy is crucial. One coding mistake might have serious repercussions, such as erroneous treatment or refused insurance claims.

Why is critical analysis crucial for medical coders?

Medical coders must be able to analyze medical data and make educated decisions regarding coding cases. Therefore analytical thinking is essential to their work. This calls for the capacity to analyze data, spot trends, and apply an understanding of medical language and coding techniques to ensure accuracy.

How important is communication in medical coding?

Communication skills are crucial for medical coders to collaborate appropriately with healthcare providers and insurance companies. Coding staff members must be able to speak professionally to guarantee that medical records are accurate and that claims are processed correctly.

How crucial is it for medical coders to understand medical terminology?

Medical coders must be familiar with medical terminology because it forms the basis of appropriate coding. To correctly assign codes to particular diagnoses and procedures, coders must be able to comprehend and use medical terminology.

Why is it crucial for medical coders to stay current on changes to coding standards and laws?

Medical coders should be informed of any changes to coding standards and guidelines since they significantly impact compliance and accuracy. To guarantee that their work is accurate and current, coders must keep up with changes in legislation, documentation needs, and other laws.

What part does technology play in the medical coding process?

Technology is crucial to medical coding because it allows coders to manage massive volumes of healthcare data and assign codes promptly and precisely. Coding software and tools can make the coding process more efficient and accurate.

How can medical coders maintain organization and efficiently handle their workload?
Medical coders can utilize checklists, calendars, and task lists to organize and manage their workload. To guarantee that work is finished on time and precisely, they can also prioritize their assignments based on due dates and priority and assign jobs as necessary.

How can medical coders make sure they are ethically coding?
Medical coders can ensure they are coding ethically by adhering to industry standards and guidelines, protecting patient privacy, and avoiding dishonest or abusive coding techniques. They must also keep up with any modifications to the healthcare industry's rules and laws governing security and privacy.

How can medical coders hone their problem-solving abilities?
Medical coders can practice examining medical records and finding patterns and irregularities to hone their problem-solving abilities. They can also ask more seasoned programmers for advice, take part in continuing education courses, and reflect on their performance to determine where they can improve.

Why is having a good work ethic necessary for medical coders?
Medical coders must have a strong work ethic to complete their work accurately and effectively. They must be able to fulfill deadlines, interact with people well, and conduct themselves at all times highly professional.

What part does cooperation play in medical coding?
Because medical coders must work closely with healthcare providers, insurance firms, and other stakeholders to ensure that medical records are accurate and that claims are processed appropriately, collaboration is crucial in medical coding. To make sure that everyone engaged is working toward the same goal, coders must be able to communicate clearly and collaborate.

How can medical coders control their stress levels?
Medical coders can control their stress levels by taking daily breaks, engaging in stress-reduction exercises like deep breathing or meditation, and keeping a healthy work-life balance. To avoid feeling overloaded, creating reasonable goals and deadlines and prioritizing work can also be beneficial.

How can medical coders make sure their work is of a high standard?
Medical coders should ensure their work is of high quality by being informed on coding standards and norms, double-checking their codes for accuracy, and asking their colleagues or superiors for feedback. They can also participate in ongoing training and education to advance their abilities and expertise.

What advice would you provide to someone just starting in the profession of medical coding?
Seeking mentorship or advice from seasoned coders, taking part in continuing education and training programs, and developing a network of business contacts are all advice for rookie medical coders. Along with patience and persistence, it's crucial to keep up with changes to coding standards and rules.

How can medical coders make sure they satisfy the requirements of their customers or employers?
Medical coders can ensure they satisfy their needs by successfully communicating with their customers or employers, delivering accurate and timely coding, and being receptive to criticism and concerns. They can also cooperate to find areas that need development and provide solutions that satisfy the demands of stakeholders.

Questions on Specialization opportunities

What are some of the medical coding specializations?
Cardiology, oncology, orthopedics, pediatrics, and emergency medicine are a few specialties within medical coding. Medical coders can gain competence and enhance their job prospects by specializing in a particular field.

What are the advantages of focusing on a specific branch of medical coding?
Medical coding specialization can open up prospects for career progression, increased pay, and better job satisfaction. Also, it can aid coders in becoming authorities in a particular field and gaining a more profound comprehension of coding rules and laws.

How do medical coders select their area of specialization?
Medical coders can select a specialty by weighing their interests, abilities, and experience. To identify which thing could be the best fit, they can also conduct a study on other specialties and consult with experts in the field.

What typical specialization certificates are available for medical coders?
The Certified Cardiology Coder (CCC), Certified Professional Coder - Hospital (CPC-H), and Certified Orthopedic Surgery Coder are a few examples of standard specialty certifications for medical coders (COSC). These credentials show mastery in a specific branch of medical coding.

How do medical coders become certified in their specific fields?
Medical coders can earn specialist certificates by completing a certification program and passing a test. Professional organizations or educational institutions may offer certification programs, often concentrating on a particular area of medical coding.

What are the future employment prospects for medical coders with specialized certifications?
Due to their established medical coding skills, medical coders with specialized certificates may have better employment opportunities and income possibilities. According to the Bureau of Labor Statistics, medical records and health information technologists' employment is expected to increase by 8% between 2019 and 2029, faster than the average for all occupations.

How can medical coders keep up with developments in their field of expertise?
Attending conferences and workshops, participating in online forums and discussion groups, and reading trade magazines can help medical coders stay current on developments in their fields of expertise. Also, they can network with other industry experts and look for further training and education possibilities.

What difficulties do medical coders in specialty fields face?
Working with complex medical data, remaining current on changes in coding guidelines and laws, and handling a lot of work are some of the problems medical coders face in specialty areas. They might also need to collaborate closely with healthcare professionals to guarantee that records are accurate and comprehensive.

How many medical coders focus on coding for a specific hospital or healthcare organization?
By getting familiar with the unique coding practices and software platforms used by each medical facility or organization, medical coders can specialize in coding for that particular facility or organization. They can also communicate successfully with healthcare providers and insurance companies to ensure that records are accurate and that claims are processed correctly.

What advice would you provide medical coders who are thinking about specializing?
Medical coders thinking of specializing should study various specialties, assess their abilities and interests, look for mentorship or advice from more seasoned coders, and participate in training and education programs for continuing education. Moreover, networking with other industry experts and looking for professional development opportunities might be beneficial.

Questions on Successful career paths

What are some typical misunderstandings regarding a job in medical coding?
One widespread myth is that medical coding is a simple job that doesn't call for any specialized training or certification. It calls for technical education and a profound familiarity with medical jargon, anatomy, and physiology.

How may a person without medical training begin a career in medical coding?
While having a medical background is advantageous, it is not necessarily required to begin working in medical coding. Numerous programs provide instruction and certification to people with various educational backgrounds.

What abilities are crucial for a successful career in medical coding?
Successful medical coding requires a keen eye for detail, critical thinking, and the capacity to pick things up fast and adapt.

What is the typical wage for a medical coder?
In May 2020, the median annual pay for medical records and health information technologists (which includes medical coders) was $44,090, according to the Bureau of Labor Statistics.

What effects has technology had on the medical coding industry?
Technology has significantly changed medical coding because it is now more accurate and efficient. The coding procedure has been streamlined, and the possibility of errors has decreased, thanks to electronic health data and coding software.

How can medical coders keep abreast of modifications to coding standards and laws?
Medical coders can keep abreast of modifications to coding standards and laws by taking continuing education courses, joining professional associations, and often reading trade journals.

What are some typical difficulties encountered by medical coders at work?
Medical coders frequently struggle with dealing with complicated medical vocabulary, remaining current with evolving coding standards, and managing a heavy workload.

What are some possible professions for medical coders?
Medical billing specialists, medical records managers, medical coding supervisors, and coding compliance auditors are among the possible job pathways for medical coders.

How crucial is precision in medical coding?
Medical coding requires exceptional accuracy since even minor mistakes can significantly impact patients, healthcare professionals, and insurance companies.

What are some tactics for developing one's medical coding career?
Further certifications, advanced study in health information management, and looking for leadership possibilities within one's firm are all ways to develop one's career in medical coding.

CONCLUSION

With our exploration of medical coding coming to an end, it is clear that this intricate yet crucial facet of the healthcare sector is crucial. This book provides a solid foundation for understanding and using medical coding principles, procedures, and tactics.

Throughout the book, we have examined the historical and modern context of medical coding, its practical applications, and the governing rules and regulations that set its standards. Aside from discussing the fundamental competencies and career paths for aspiring medical coders, we have also covered modern tools and techniques that promote efficiency.

Medical coding specialists must be ready to change and advance with new technology, rules, and industry requirements in today's quickly changing healthcare environment. Medical coders can ensure their abilities are current and valuable in the face of change by constantly learning new information and remaining updated with industry trends.

Lastly, this book will prove invaluable in your quest to understand the nuances of medical coding. If you are a novice learning the coding industry, an expert coder looking to advance your career, or a healthcare professional looking to improve your organization's coding procedures, we wish you success. The realm of medical coding is challenging and rewarding, and I wish you a successful, fruitful, and informative journey.

YOUR EXTRA STUDY AIDS

Dear reader, esteemed reader, If you're perusing these lines, you've embarked on a fascinating journey of knowledge, and we're thrilled to be part of your adventure.

Your insights are pure gold!
Your thoughts, experiences, and feedback on the content you're holding are absolutely invaluable to us. We'd love for you to share your journey with our book on Amazon. Whether it's a specific section that struck a chord with you or the overall voyage through the pages that's enriched your understanding, your perspective is priceless. Sharing your thoughts not only aids fellow readers in their exploration but also inspires us, the authors, to continuously elevate and enrich your reading experience.

Delve into Our Special Surprise!
In heartfelt appreciation, we've curated a unique surprise just for you. Here's what awaits:

- **Audiobook,** to be listened to whenever you want.
- A digital **book: "CPC Exam Study Guide"** so you can go over everything about your career.
- A digital **book: "Medical Terminology".**
- *NOTE.* This book has also been made into **+600 digital flashcards with pictures**, and you can use it to *repeat and memorize.*
- **50 Digital Flashcards with practical examples** of how these terms are used in medical billing and coding practice. Each flashcard describes a **different pathology or medical condition**, with a unique case illustrating **how that manifests itself and how it can be treated.** Thus, you will have a <u>**wide range of knowledge**</u> and be able to apply it to different clinical situations.

You can track your progress and conveniently and interactively memorize the most important terms and concepts! Download to your device: **Anki APP or AnkiDroid**, or enter the web page and register free of charge. Then import the files we have given you as a gift and use the flashcards whenever and wherever you want to study and track your progress.

Seamless Enrichment, No Strings Attached!
Enclosed below, you'll discover an exclusive QR CODE, offering direct access to additional content crafted exclusively for your enjoyment. No cumbersome subscriptions or personal details required. This is our genuine gift to you, aimed at supporting your ongoing learning journey.

If you encounter any hurdles while accessing or downloading the content, please don't hesitate to reach out to us at **info.testbookreader@gmail.com.**
We're here to lend a helping hand.

Warm regards and best wishes for your continued success,
We eagerly await your feedback!
Thank you!

Made in the USA
Columbia, SC
20 September 2024